Lord Teach me How to Pray!

Alfred O. Tagoe

Lord Teach me How to Pray!
Alfred O. Tagoe

ISBN 978-0615778723

Copyright © 2013 by Voice of Revival Ministries

All rights reserved. No part of this book may be reproduced or transmitted in any form or by any means without written permission from the author.

Voice of Revival Ministries
5696 Earnings Dr,
Columbus, OH, 43232.
www.voiceofrevival.net

Printed in the United States of America

Unless otherwise noted, all Scripture is taken from the New King James Version copyright © 1982 Thomas Nelson, Inc. Used by permission. All rights reserved.
*Scripture text in bold or italics is the emphasis of the author.

TABLE OF CONTENTS:

Dedication & Acknowledgements 4

Foreword 6

Endorsement 9

Prologue 11

Introduction 17

Chapter 1: Prayer of Acknowledgement 22
Connecting with God's Paternity

Chapter 2: Prayer of Adoration 35
Connecting with Divine Personality

Chapter 3: Prayer of Intercession 53
Connecting with Divine Partnership

Chapter 4: Prayer of Commitment 85
Connecting to Divine Purpose

Chapter 5: Prayer of Petition 103
Connecting with Divine Provision

Chapter 6: Prayer of Confession 117
Connecting with Divine Pardon

Chapter 7: Prayer of Covering 131
Connecting with Divine Protection

Epilogue 151

DEDICATION

I would like to dedicate this book to the two most influential women in my life: my wife, Angelina Tagoe and my mother Hariet Tagoe. I also dedicate this book to all those prayer warriors whose unceasing prayers continue to shape the course of history and nations.

ACKNOWLEDGMNENTS

First of all I would like to thank God, the Father, the Son, and the Holy Spirit who provided me the strength, resolve, and direction to accomplish this task. To my loving wife, Angie, words cannot express my gratitude for your love and support throughout this journey. To my children Jezzy, Jaeda, and Joshua, you are all a blessing to me. To Brondon Mathis, George Agbonson, and Evelyn Turnbull, I thank you for your constant inspiration and motivation to take on the task of writing books. Finally, to everyone who helped in any way to proof-read, edit, and publish this book, I owe you a debt of gratitude.

FOREWORD

Jesus' disciples asked Him to teach them how to pray. He taught them to preach, cast out devils, heal the sick and do many other things, but one thing they were passionate about was how to pray. Ironically, many believers today don't ask the Lord to teach them to pray. Books on prayer are the least patronized and prayer conferences are the least attended. Most believers don't pray. Those who pray, pray amiss and mix sin with long and laborious prayers. The time for heart-felt and God-centred prayer is now. The times we live in are dangerous and decisive. We cannot continue to move away from prayer and constantly engage in religious exercises that satisfy the flesh and tickle the intellect but have no spiritual value.

Pastor Alfred Tagoe has not written a theoretical book on prayer. This book, "Lord, teach me how to pray", is prayer by itself. Alfred has been engaged in travailing and prevailing prayer for years and knows how to pray. His experience in prayer and knowledge of the Word of God, qualify him to write on the subject of prayer. I was personally, inspired to pray more when I read the manuscript. I have no doubt that this book will release a prayer revival in your spirit.

Adoration, intercession, commitment, petition, confession and covering are extensively treated as the areas of prayer you must cover in your prayer life. Praying involves more than just speaking words to God. It is complete devotion to God, which involves holiness, obedience and active interaction with Him. Those who are holy are drawn into the holy place to pray but sinners are driven out of the prayer closet. One's lifestyle cannot be divorced from one's prayer life. An individual who lives in sin cannot pray and even if he or she pretends to pray, he or she cannot last in prayer.

Alfred Tagoe urges every believer to engage in prayer. Prayer is not the vocation of only pastors and those in ministry. It is the vocation of every believer. Prayer is the believer's life – it is the reason for living and the means for living. If we don't pray we die spiritually and if we are spiritually dead we cannot pray. The "death of prayer" in the Church is the number one reason for its powerlessness and inability to fulfil the Great Commission. Many believers are unfulfilled in life because they don't discover God's will for their lives through prayer.

Alfred Tagoe says in this book, "Through prayer, intercession and strategic evangelism, God has mandated His Church to infiltrate and subdue these strata of society to reflect His character and values." It is impossible for the will of God to be done on earth without prayer. We cannot be the salt of the earth without prayer. Prayer is the believer's breath and the key to spiritual power. There is a prayer revival in some parts of the world but most of the Christian world has failed to catch the fire. Misplaced priorities and worldliness have combined to drive believers out of the prayer closet. It is time to return to the place of prayer.

A man who knows how to pray, Alfred Tagoe shows us the way in this book. You hold in your hands the key to a new dimension of prayer. As you read it, you will cultivate a prayer lifestyle that will keep you in the Father's bosom and draw all men to Him.

Rev. Eastwood Anaba
President
Eastwood Anaba Ministries (EAM)

ENDORSEMENT

I have known Apostle Alfred Tagoe for years now as a man who is a quiver in God's hand because of the unusual grace and revelation of prayer bestowed on him. I call him the Apostle of Prayer and Reformation because God has endowed him for such a time as this when the Body of Christ needs revival. Prayer will be the platform for such revival and transformation. There is no other person than Apostle Alfred Tagoe whose writing will trigger the fire of revival in our lives and churches. I know you will never remain the same reading this book.

Dr. George Agbonson
President
Christ Restoration Ministries International

"God does nothing but in answer to prayers of the saints" a wise man once said. Also true is the fact that every major move of God on earth is often preceded by His stirring up a remnant who He anoints to pray. Many however do pray but pray amiss. This classic piece put together by the author, is a perfect tool for every serious minded intercessor who feels called to pray the heart of our God into the realm of reality in this generation and that which is yet to come. I strongly recommend it.

Rev Sam Adeyemi.
Senior Pastor
Overcomers Christian Center

This book on Prayer by Alfred Tagoe is a must for those that desire a deeper more intimate relationship with the father in prayer. This book will give you 7 prayers to pray to unlock the person, presence, and power of Christ in your life. I highly recommend it.

Brondon Mathis
Founder
Yeshua Life Ministries

From the opening chapter to the last word, Apostle Alfred Tagoe offers a fresh perspective on prayer. He corrects many of our misunderstandings about prayer and creates a step-by-step blueprint for us to follow. He takes us from embracing our Father's unlimited resources to connecting with His divine protection. Along the way, Alfred issues a stern command, "Stop Complaining: Pray!" Then he draws us back to the biblical formula of simply asking and receiving. Regardless of your level of prayer development, this book is bound to improve your prayer life.

Sandee Hemphill- Prophet
Founder
Pray Columbus

PROLOGUE:

No greater request has fallen from the lips of mortal men who will soon transform their world and generation, than the request of the twelve disciples of Jesus to their Master; "Lord, teach us to pray..." It is noteworthy that this request was made after their Master had completed a season or session of personal prayer.

Luke 11:1: *"And it came to pass, that, as he was praying in a certain place, when he ceased, one of his disciples said unto him, **Lord, teach us to pray**, as John also taught his disciples."* (Emphasis mine)

I have always been intrigued by this request from these men who had the privilege and opportunity to ask the Lord for anything. They had witnessed Him wipe the blindness off of Bartimeus' eyes; cleansed the leprosy from the leper; caused the flow of blood to cease from the woman with the issue of blood (who by the way, had this problem for twelve years) and other healings He had performed. I have therefore wondered why they did not ask Him to teach them how to heal the sick. They had seen Him cast out devils on many occasions and had actually been rebuked by Him once for being unable to cast the devil out of the young man, and yet given the opportunity for a request, they did not ask Him to teach them how to cast out devils.

They were in the boat with Him when the storms raged and their lives were in jeopardy. Upon waking Jesus up from a deep sleep, they witnessed Him as he rebuked the storm with one word from His mouth and seen the winds ceased and the ocean calmed, yet they did not request that He teach them how to calm hurricanes and tornadoes. Once while they were out to sea and Jesus was still onshore dispersing the crowd, they were experiencing hurricane type winds and saw their Master coming to them walking on the water. I would think that given the opportunity to request for anything, they might want to know the secret of how to walk on water. There are many other extraordinary feats that these disciples had witnessed their Master accomplish, like raising the dead and feeding the multitudes with a few loaves of bread and fish, and yet the one thing they wanted Him to teach them was 'how to pray'.

I believe the reason why the disciples were more interested in being taught how to pray is because their Lord and Master,

Jesus, had modeled a lifestyle of prayer before them; a lifestyle that put intimacy and communion with His Father at a premium. They recognized that the source of His power could be directly associated with His prayer life.

It is very important to note, in spite of what many theologians may say, that Jesus did not heal the sick, cast out devils, raise the dead, and walk on water just because of His deity or Divinity. He accomplished those supernatural acts because as a Man He relied totally on the Holy Ghost's ability to anoint and empower Him, (Luke 4:18 & Acts 10:38).

> *The key to His power was His prayer!*

Luke 4:18: *"The **Spirit of the Lord** is upon me, because he hath **anointed** me to preach the gospel to the poor; he hath sent me to heal the brokenhearted, to preach deliverance to the captives, and recovering of sight to the blind, to set at liberty them that are bruised."* (Emphasis mine)

Act 10:38: *"How God **anointed Jesus of Nazareth** with the Holy Ghost and with power: who went about doing good, and healing all that were oppressed of the devil; for God was with him."* (Emphasis mine)

He was able to depend on the Holy Spirit through His constant communion with the Father through prayer. Jesus made it clear that He could do nothing on His own accord except what He saw His Father do.

John 5:19: *"Then answered Jesus and said unto them, Verily, verily, I say unto you, **The Son can do nothing of himself**, but what he seeth the Father do: for what things soever he doeth, these also doeth the Son likewise."* (Emphasis mine)

A cursory look at the life of the Master on earth will reveal a Man in constant communion with His Father in Heaven. One of the earliest examples of Jesus praying is recorded in the Gospel according to Mark. Jesus had just had one of the greatest meetings any of our contemporary Evangelists will be proud of. The whole city had gathered in front of the house of Simon Peter and many sick people were healed and the demon possessed were delivered, (Mark 1:32-34). This is the type of revival meeting many today yearn for and if it happens would do everything possible to keep it going for days if not weeks; irrespective of whether that would be God's will or not. However, in the midst of such ministry explosion and "success", we have a glimpse into the most important aspect of Jesus' life; the one thing that made Him tick… IT WAS HIS PRAYER LIFE!

Mark 1: 35: *"And in the morning, rising up a great while before day, he went out, and departed into a solitary place, and **there prayed**."* (Emphasis mine)

The disciples of course, just like many of us who are moved and fascinated with the fruit and manifestation of ministry came looking for him in the morning to continue the "show" or see him operate His power ministry. It must have been a disappointment but a life lesson when they were informed by the Lord that He was not continuing the "revival meeting".

Mark 1:36: *"And Simon and they that were with him followed after him. And when they had found him, they said unto him, All men seek for thee. And he said unto them, Let us go into the next towns, that I may preach there also: for therefore came I forth."*

Instead of being moved by the "success" of the previous night's meeting and hence looking for a repeat performance, the Lord had received new instruction while in communion with the Father about His assignment. It was time to move on to the next towns and villages.

Prayer had so much influence in the Lord's life that His disciples could not help but to notice it. Obviously, they concluded that if the sinless Son of God who is the Creator of the Universe and upholds all things by the Word of His power needed to pray and depend on the help of the Holy Spirit during His earthly ministry; they should follow suit. Think about it: how much more should they pray and depend upon the Holy Spirit. How much more do we today need to pray and depend upon the strength, wisdom, and power of the Holy Spirit to accomplish the assignments and commissions given to us by God? Jesus said we would do greater works than He did because He is with the Father. Well, I believe that to do greater works, we must first also do greater prayer; for greater prayer will produce greater power for greater works!

INTRODUCTION

Jesus' response to His disciple's request, "Lord, teach us to pray" has been characterized by many through many generations as the "Lord's Prayer". It has also been one of the most memorized and recited prayers of all time. For one, rather than call this the "Lord's Prayer", it would be more accurate and appropriate to call it the "Disciple's Prayer" since Jesus Himself did not pray it but taught His disciples to use it to pray. The "Lord's Prayer" can actually be located in the Gospel of John, Chapter 17, where Jesus' High Priestly prayer for His Church just before His journey to the cross is recorded. Secondly, Jesus did not intend for it to become just another prayer to be memorized and recited, even though reciting it with faith and understanding would yield great results.

Ultimately, Jesus was responding to His disciples' request to be tutored in the art of prayer since they had observed how much prayer was at the core of their teacher's life and ministry. Jesus was giving them a formula, if you will, of prayer. In other words, His response to His disciples should be seen as a blue print or model to be used when we are engaged with God in prayer, rather than a flippant recital we use as an excuse for real prayer.

A careful review of His response with the help of the Holy Spirit will reveal a step by step approach to God through prayer, and also a valuable resource of the different types of prayer we employ to receive specific answers and results. The great Apostle Paul admonished the Church in Ephesus to pray with ALL manner or kinds of prayer.

Ephesians 6:18: *"Praying always with all prayer and supplication in the Spirit, and watching thereunto with all perseverance and supplication for all saints."*

In Mathew 16, Jesus spoke to His disciples in general, and to Peter in particular that He would give them the KEYS to the Kingdom.

Matt. 16:19: *"And I will give unto thee the keys of the kingdom of heaven: and whatsoever thou shalt bind on earth shall be bound in heaven: and whatsoever thou shalt loose on earth shall be loosed in heaven."*

The purpose of giving them the keys was to bind and loose, which indicates prayer activity. In other words prayer is the means by which we activate or use the keys to gain access to those things in the Kingdom reserved for Gods people on earth, (loosing); and also deny access to the adversary from perpetuating his diabolical agenda on earth, (binding).

It is important to understand that "keys" represent authority and access. For example, to possess a key to a bank vault indicates that you have the authority to access the contents of that vault, at the same time, ensuring that access is denied all other persons without the key. It is interesting also to note that Jesus did not say He was giving the disciples (and by extension us; His disciples today,) the "key" to the Kingdom, but rather the "keys" to the Kingdom. This implies therefore that there are different keys that access different aspects or provisions in the Kingdom of God. In a large mansion, there are many different rooms and hence doors or access points to those rooms. In many cases, there are different keys that lock or unlock access to specific rooms in the mansion. The key that grants access to the garage where the Porsche in parked is different to the key that opens the door to the library. If one tries to access the library full of its wealth of knowledge with the key to the garage, he or she will be denied access and thus become frustrated even though he or she possesses ALL the keys to the house.

I believe the "keys" represent different types of prayers that we need to employ to access our different needs and desires. I also believe that one of the reasons many "disciples" today are not seeing results or receiving answers to their prayers is because they try to use the wrong type of prayer to access a particular need. In other words, they attempt to use the key to the garage to gain access to the contents of the library. Would it not be easier if we knew what key or prayer to use to access the many benefits of the Kingdom?

Jesus made it clear that He has given us ALL the keys; but knowing which key to use where, how, and when is as important, if not more important, than just knowing you possess the keys. Knowing what and when to bind and loose is very important. Therefore, knowing HOW to pray is the greatest lesson we can ever learn from the Master. No wonder it became the greatest request His disciples made of Him, "Lord, teach us how to pray".

This appeal should also become our greatest desire and request if we are going to enjoy the glorious lifestyle in the Kingdom of God.

In the following chapters of this manuscript, we are going to discover and explore seven different types of prayer; and explain how and why each one works when prayed by themselves; but also how powerful they are when prayed in sequence and in concert with one another. This journey of discovery will transform your prayer life from one of mundane repetitiveness, to one of excitement and joy in the presence of God. My prayer is that the Body of Christ will once again cry out to the Lord, like the Disciples did over two thousand years ago "Lord, teach us to pray".

Before you begin reading this book however, you have to ask yourself if you are a disciple of Jesus. Are you born-again? If the answer is "No", I simply recommend for you to pray the following prayer:

Father, I come to you just as I am in the Name of Your Son Jesus. I acknowledge that I am a sinner and in need of a Savior. I believe with my heart that Jesus died on the cross for my sins and that He resurrected on the third day for my justification. Lord Jesus I ask you to come into my heart; become my Lord and Savior; and fill me with your Holy Spirit. Thank you Father for answering my prayer!

If you sincerely prayed this prayer you are now a child of God and a disciple of Jesus. Please find a good Bible-based, Spirit-filled Church where your faith will be nurtured. You are now also ready to learn how to communicate with your Father through prayer. God bless you!

CHAPTER 1
Prayer of Acknowledgment
(Connecting with Divine Paternity)

Our Father which art in heaven… (Luke 11:2a)

Jesus begins His instruction on prayer by reintroducing God to His disciples as Father. These disciples had been raised up in the Jewish tradition which taught them based on the Torah (Five books of Moses or the Law of Moses) to approach God with fear and trembling. They were even careful not to misspell His Name YAHWEH and definitely would not think themselves worthy to approach Him as Father. One of the issues that aggravated the religious leaders against Jesus was His constant reference to God as His Father and Himself as the Son of God. To them it was a sign of disrespect as Jesus was claiming to be "like" God and also claiming to have a personal relationship with Him. The idea that God could be their Father was mostly foreign to these disciples. It was a privilege they felt unqualified and unworthy of.

Even though most of us in today's generation may take it for granted, the Fatherhood of God was one concept the Jews could not easily receive but was the greatest revelation that Jesus came to introduce to them. One of the most important reasons Jesus came to die on the cross was so that God would not just be "God" but also "Father". He suffered, bled, and died so that His God would be our God, and His Father would be our Father; that is why I believe one of the most important verses in the bible is John 20:17, where Jesus sums up His mission when He encountered Mary at the tomb after His resurrection.

John 20:17: *"Jesus saith unto her, Touch me not; for I am not yet ascended to my Father: but go to my brethren, and say unto them, I ascend unto **my Father, and your Father;** and to my God, and your God."* (Emphasis mine)

God's intention has always been to reveal Himself and relate to His people not only as "God" but as "Father" or "Pater" which means "originator of life". God as Father therefore has the connotation of one who protects, provides, and is a sustainer of the life He initiates. We are His "offspring", as Paul declared to the Philosophers in Athens (Acts 17). This God, who the disciples knew as Jehovah, desired a personal relationship with His people, because you see, they were not just His "people" but also His "sons and daughters".

John 1:12 & 13: *"But as many as received him, to them gave he power to become the sons of God, even to them that believe on his name: Which were born, not of blood, nor of the will of the flesh, nor of the will of man, but of God."*

2 Corinthians 6:17 & 18: *"Wherefore come out from among them, and be ye separate, saith the Lord, and touch not the unclean thing; and I will receive you, And will be a **Father unto you,** and **ye shall be my sons and daughters**, saith the Lord Almighty."* (Emphasis mine)

It is no wonder that the Apostle John after years of walking in intimacy with the Lord still could not get over the fact that the greatest expression of God's love for us was to make us His children.

1John 3:1: *"Behold, what manner of love the Father hath bestowed upon us, that we should be called the sons of God: therefore the world knoweth us not, because it knew him not."*

So we see that it was very important for the disciple's to understand and acknowledge who it was they were praying to. Jesus had to make it clear that He was their Father; and not any kind of father, but the One who lives in Heaven. This was also very important for Jesus to differentiate between this Father, who is in Heaven, and their or our earthly fathers. I believe there are two main reasons why this differentiation is important:

1. **Unlimited Resources:**

We have to understand that as children of God, our Heavenly Father has unlimited resources unlike our earthly fathers. This generates faith in our hearts to know that no matter what our need is or whatever circumstance we may have; when we approach His throne of Grace He is more than able to deal with our situation. No matter how wealthy, powerful, and influential your earthly father may be, he is still limited in many ways to what he can do for you. On one hand, your earthly father is limited by time and space, and hence cannot always be with you to guide, protect, or help you. On the other hand, you have a Heavenly Father who says He will never leave you or forsake you. He will be with you in trouble and has power to deliver you out of trouble.

Psalm 91:14 & 15: *"Because he hath set his love upon me, therefore will I deliver him: I will set him on high, because he hath known my name. He shall call upon me, and I will answer him: **I***

will be with him in trouble; I will deliver him, *and honour him."* (Emphasis mine)

Psalm 46: 1: *"God is our refuge and strength, a very present help in trouble."*

Secondly, earthly fathers have inadequate means simply because earth's resources and human abilities and capacities are limited. However, heaven's resources are abundant, and our Heavenly Father's abilities and capacities are unmatched, unparalleled, and unlimited.

2 Peter 1:3: *"According as **his divine power** hath given unto us all things that pertain unto life and godliness, through the knowledge of him that hath called us to glory and virtue: Whereby are given unto us exceeding great and precious promises: that by these ye might be partakers of the divine nature, having escaped the corruption that is in the world through lust."* (Emphasis mine)

"His divine power…" can be translated as "His unlimited resources…" In fact, our God, (Father) owns the cattle upon a thousand hills. The silver and gold is His. "The earth is the Lords and the fullness thereof…" declares the Psalmist. Since He has unlimited resources, He can and will provide ALL your needs according to His riches in glory by Christ Jesus, (Philippians 4:19).

Jesus wants us to know that the Father we approach in prayer has unlimited

> *Our Heavenly Father's abilities are unmatched, unparalleled, and unlimited.*

resources unlike the earthly father we have dealt with or dealing with right now; and irrespective of how rich or poor; strong or weak; influential or non-influential they are; they cannot be compared with our Heavenly Father. He can be trusted to answer every prayer and provide for every need.

2. **Distorted Viewpoint:**

I have met and ministered to men and women who (due to the unhealthy relationship they have had with their earthly fathers) have a distorted view of their Heavenly Father. It breaks my heart, and I believe more so the heart of the Father, that due to a father's abusive relationship and mistreatment of his son or daughter; the child grows up and has a perception of God the Father that is distorted, perverted, and corrupted based on that relationship. There are many born-again, Spirit-filled men and women who are unable to really connect with God as Father simply because, whether they realize it or not, their perception of Him as a Father is deeply rooted and based in the type of relationship they had with their earthly father.

It is heartbreaking to see and talk to women especially, who don't believe their worth because they either did not have a father to affirm their beauty and worth, or worse they had a father (or father figure) who routinely abused them verbally, physically, or/and sexually. They therefore live their lives with shame and have a low self-esteem, seeking approval and affirmation from other men (or father figures). For some, if not most, it leads them on the path of destruction as they either end up in abusive relationships because they don't think they are worth much anyway; or to a lifestyle of promiscuity and prostitution since they often end up blaming themselves for the actions or inactions of the man they called father; hence accepting that lifestyle as who they were meant to be. Some have found themselves into a homosexual lifestyle since they have made up their minds not to have any relationship with another man. Let me make it plain when I say homosexual: I am referring to either a man or woman who cannot receive or give love appropriately because the love of a father or father figure did not portray their role as a father in a responsible manner. Instead of being the one who should have given their child their identity, they robbed them of their identity; leaving them forever seeking love, acceptance and purpose.

Jesus came to set the captives free, and if you or someone you know have been held hostage by this spirit of rejection, manifesting itself in these vices, (as a result of the kind of relationship you had or did not have with your earthly father,) it is time to be free.

It is amazing that even after being saved, these strongholds of rejection, worthlessness, and low self-esteem still persist in the lives of those who have had negative relationships with earthly fathers, and thus, are translated into their relationship with their Heavenly Father. It is difficult for them to receive His unconditional love. They put up defenses in their hearts because they do not want to be wounded, abused, or disappointed by any one again; and invariably also shut up their hearts to God, their Heavenly Father, for fear that He will also disappoint them.

Others try hard, through the works of the flesh, to please God in order to receive His affection and approval instead of simply accepting the finished work of Christ on the cross on their behalf. They need to realize that the Father loves them furiously and unconditionally; and has already approved, and affirmed them. If you doubt your worth to God and your worth in life, God simply asks you to look on the cross of Calvary, for there He paid the ultimate price of redemption through His son's death in order to have a relationship with you as a Father.

When Jesus taught His disciples to begin their prayer by first acknowledging the "Father who is in Heaven", he is in essence asking them to renew their minds and focus not on the relationship (whether good or bad) that exists between them and their earthly fathers. Instead, the focus should be on the relationship that exists between them and the Father who "so loved the world that He gave His only Begotten Son…" (John 3:16). This great Father, the One who not only provides for their every need but also disciplines them because He loves them resides in a place that is superior to anything they have ever known. God wants his children who have accepted his love and have submitted themselves to His chastening which only makes us mature, to one day dwell with Him forever. An earthly father can never provide an eternal dwelling place for their child... only God the Father can.

Hebrews 12:5 - 10: *"And ye have forgotten the exhortation which speaketh unto you as unto children, My son, despise not thou the chastening of the Lord, nor faint when thou art rebuked of him:* **For whom the Lord loveth he chasteneth, and scourgeth every son whom he receiveth**. *If ye endure chastening, God dealeth with you as with sons; for what son is he whom the father chasteneth not? But if ye be without chastisement, whereof all are partakers, then are ye bastards, and not sons. Furthermore we have had fathers of our flesh which corrected us, and we gave them reverence: shall we not much rather be in subjection unto the Father of spirits, and live? For they verily for a few days chastened us after their own pleasure; but he for our profit, that we might be partakers of his holiness."* (Emphasis mine)

Even our earthly fathers, who the bible refers to as "evil," know how to give us good things, how much more would our Heavenly Father give us good things.

Matt. 7:9 – 11: *"Or what man is there of you, whom if his son ask bread, will he give him a stone? Or if he ask a fish, will he give him a serpent? If ye then, being evil, know how to give good gifts unto your children,* **how much more shall your Father which is in heaven give good things to them that ask him***?"* (Emphasis mine)

So let us come boldly to the throne room of our Heavenly Father in prayer without hesitation, and without reservation and declare with confidence, "Our Father, Who is in Heaven…" Your Father is longing to hear your prayer and answer it. He is waiting with open arms to embrace you into His loving, joyful, and peaceful presence. He wants to heal your wounds, soothe your pain, and minister to your every need according to His will. Don't wait another moment; don't hesitate. Let us go into His presence together and pray this prayer of acknowledgement with me.

LET US PRAY:

My dear Heavenly Father, I thank you for revealing to me that you are my Father who loves and cares for me. Please forgive me for the times when I have not approached you with boldness and confidence as my Father because of fear and lack of faith generated as result of wrong perceptions of who you are. I now realize that you truly love me and will not harm nor reject me because of my failures. Please continue to reveal your fatherhood heart unto me, and remove anything in me such as fear, doubt, and low self-esteem that will hinder the full manifestation of your love to me and through me. I love you Daddy! Amen!

CHAPTER 2

Prayer of Adoration

(Connecting with Divine Personality)

Hallowed be thy name... (Luke 11:2b)

After Jesus reconnects us to His Father by teaching us to acknowledge His Fatherhood with all its implications and benefits, He then wants us to worship or adore the Father. God, our Heavenly Father desires and deserves our adoration and worship. In fact, there are two kinds of people the bible makes clear that God is seeking: Intercessors and Worshippers. In the Book of Ezekiel, God declared that He seeks for an Intercessor;

Ezekiel 22: 30*: "And I sought for a man among them, that should make up the hedge, and stand in the gap before me for the land, that I should not destroy it: but I found none."*

Jesus in His dealing with the woman at the well of Jacob in the Gospel of John Chapter 4, made it clear that God, the Father is seeking Worshippers.

John 4:21 - 24*: "Jesus saith unto her, Woman, believe me, the hour cometh, when ye shall neither in this mountain, nor yet at Jerusalem, worship the Father. Ye worship ye know not what: we* *know what we worship: for salvation is of the Jews. But the hour cometh, and now is, when the true worshippers shall worship the Father in spirit and in truth for the Father seeketh such to worship him. God is a Spirit: and they that worship him must worship him in spirit and in truth."*

In this eye opening encounter with the Samaritan woman, we see how Jesus reintroduces and connects her with the Fatherhood of God which again was a foreign concept in her culture.

What is in a Name?

Jesus taught His disciples to "hallow" the Father's Name. The Greek Lexicon for "Hallow" implies to "make holy" or "venerate" which also means to revere or worship. In other words, Jesus does not want us in our prayer to only acknowledge the Father, but to also show absolute reverence and awe at His Name. How do we proceed to do that, since for most of us a name is merely a noun given to a person, place, or thing simply to identify it and distinguish it from everything else?

Most people, especially in the Western world, don't put much substance and meaning into naming their children and sometimes they even give the same name to their children as they would their pets. Many also simply name their children after their favorite TV or sports personality without taking any interest in the meaning of that name. However, historically, names were used to describe a position or title of a person; for example a Monarch such as: Pharaoh, Caesar, and Herod etc. in other words, there is much more significance in a "name" than just an identifying and distinguishing feature.

Both the Hebrew and Greek lexicon for "name" is the same: It means, "Authority" and "Character". This signifies that the true application of a name is to project the nature, attributes, authority, and character of the person being described. That is why, unlike most people in the Western culture, people in the African and Middle-Eastern cultures who understand this concept are deliberate in giving names to their children. They appreciate the fact that the name they give their children, though it may sound strange and even sometimes cause some to scratch their heads because of the meaning, would eventually define who they become in character and in status.

The Jewish people, more than any other group in my opinion, understand and appreciate this concept. Throughout the bible, please notice how names were given and see how almost always, these names were given for a specific reason because they carried a significant meaning. Whether it was Abraham, Isaac, Jacob, Moses, Samson or Samuel, (just to name a few,) their names had significant

> *A name is to project the nature, attributes, authority, and character of a person.*

meanings and implications for what they would become and what they would do. In fact, God sometimes overruled the prerogative of the parents to assign their children's names by instructing them what name to give the child based on the specific purpose and assignment God had for that child's life. Two great examples are John (the Baptist) and Jesus (the Christ).

Luke 1:13 – 17: *"But the angel said unto him, Fear not, Zacharias: for thy prayer is heard; and thy wife Elisabeth shall bear thee a son, and thou shalt call his name John. And thou shalt have joy and gladness; and many shall rejoice at his birth. For he shall be great in the sight of the Lord, and shall drink neither wine nor strong drink; and he shall be filled with the Holy Ghost, even from his mother's womb. And many of the children of Israel shall he turn to the Lord their God. And he shall go before him in the spirit and power of Elias, to turn the hearts of the fathers to the* *children, and the disobedient to the wisdom of the just; to make ready a people prepared for the Lord."*

Likewise, before Jesus was born, these scriptures record who He was going to be:

Matt. 1:20 & 21: *"But while he thought on these things, behold, the angel of the LORD appeared unto him in a dream, saying, Joseph, thou son of David, fear not to take unto thee Mary thy wife: for that which is conceived in her is of the Holy Ghost. And she shall bring forth a son, and thou shalt call his name JESUS: for he shall save his people from their sins."*

Isaiah 9:6: *"For unto us a child is born, unto us a son is given: and the government shall be upon his shoulder: and his name shall be called Wonderful, Counselor, The mighty God, The everlasting Father, The Prince of Peace."*

I also want to show you an example in the bible where a name was associated with problems. There was a man child named Jabez who realized later in his life that the pain and sorrow he was having in his life could be directly related to the name his mother gave him. He realized that he was simply fulfilling the prophetic utterance of his name. In order to have different and better circumstances in his life, he needed to have a different name. So he wisely cried out to God for a reversal of his fortune and destiny; and God graciously heeded his call.

(King James Version) 1Chronicles 4:9 & 10: *"And Jabez was more honourable than his brethren: and his mother called his name Jabez, saying, Because I bare him with sorrow. And Jabez called on the God of Israel, saying, Oh that thou wouldest bless me indeed, and enlarge my coast, and that thine hand might be with me, and that thou wouldest keep me from evil, that it may not grieve me! And God granted him that which he requested."*

Now let us read the same text from another version: **(New International Version)**

"Jabez was more honorable than his brothers. His mother had named him Jabez, saying, "I gave birth to him in pain." Jabez cried out to the God of Israel, "Oh, that you would bless me and enlarge my territory! Let your hand be with me, and keep me from harm so that I will be free from pain." And God granted his request."

Not only did people try to change their names and hence their character or destiny, the Lord Jesus Himself took the liberty to change some of His disciples names; notably Simon (which means "a reed') who he surnamed Peter (meaning "a rock). In making the name switch, Jesus was in effect changing the very DNA of Peter by declaring to him that he will no longer be an unstable person, easily moved by the winds of circumstances and persecution. He would rather hence forth be a rock upon which the Kingdom of God could be depended on, stable and unwavering. May the Lord give you a new name based on His calling and destiny for your life!

What is Your Name?

There is an intriguing story in the bible concerning the patriarch Jacob and his encounter with God at a place called Peniel. Jacob, after years of "exile" from his home in Canaan and sojourning with his uncle Laban, was attempting to return home to reconcile with his brother Esau. This was a serious and dangerous undertaking since Esau, still bitter and angry about losing his birthright and blessing to his younger brother Jacob, was himself on his way to meet Jacob, maybe not to welcome him back home, but to kill him. When Jacob heard that his brother Esau was coming to meet him he broke out into a frantic panic; obviously fearing for his life and that of his family.

That night, after separating himself from his travelling company, a Man came and wrestled with him till the breaking of day. Let us pick up the narrative from Genesis 32;

Genesis 32:24-28: *"And Jacob was left alone; and there wrestled a man with him until the breaking of the day. And when he saw that he prevailed not against him, he touched the hollow of his* *thigh; and the hollow of Jacob's thigh was out of joint, as he wrestled with him. And he said, let me go, for the day breaketh. And he said, I will not let thee go, except thou bless me. And he said unto him, **what is thy name**? And he said, Jacob. And he said, Thy name shall be called no more Jacob, but Israel: for as a prince hast thou power with God and with men, and hast prevailed."* (Emphasis mine)

There are a couple of things I want you to see here:

1. When the Angel of God asked Jacob to let him go because of the breaking of day, Jacob responded, like we should; "I will not let you go, except you **bless** me". (Vs. 26)

2. In response, the Angel asked Jacob a question; "What is your **name**?" (Vs 27)

I believe Jacob wondered in his mind the same question I have; "what has blessing me got to do with my name?" I can hear the answer ringing from heaven, "EVERYTHING!"

As we have already established, the name of a person signifies their position, honor, and therefore character. Jacob's name literally meant "Heel-catcher" or "Supplanter" which has the connotation of one who strives and deceives to get ahead in life. Jacob, from the moment he came out of his mother's womb fulfilled the meaning of his name. He came out of the womb holding on to Esau's heels (Gen 25:26). Later in life, he would subtly convince his brother into selling his birth-right. Then he deceived his father Isaac into giving him the first-born blessing. He was shrewd and cunning with his dealings with his uncle Laban, who himself was a crafty man. All in all Jacob, even though he had the favor of God on his life, was always depending on the arm of flesh to accomplish everything.

He had finally come to the end of his own strength and needed a hand bigger and stronger than his to deliver him from the possible wrath of his brother Esau. He could not talk his way out of this situation, nor could he deceive his brother a second time; he definitely needed divine intervention.

However, he was unprepared for the Angel's response to his request for a 'blessing'. When the Angel asked him "what is your name?" he was basically asking Jacob, "what have they been calling you; because you have been fulfilling the meaning of the label placed upon you". Therefore to change the course of his life and destiny, Jacob needed a change in his DNA. He needed a name change.

Gen. 32:28: *"And he said, Thy name shall be called no more Jacob, but Israel: for as a prince hast thou power with God and with men, and hast prevailed."*

The name Israel means 'he will rule with God' or simply a 'Prince of God'. By giving him a new name, God was affirming who Jacob already was and what he was about to become and do. You see, everyone else saw Jacob as a Supplanter, and so that is also how he saw himself; but God saw him as a conquering Prince; one who prevailed with man and God. Now his name Israel would confirm who he really was. Needless to say, Jacob's life was never the same after that night of divine encounter that resulted in a name change, and furthermore resulted in a wonderful reconciliation with his brother Esau.

I AM THAT I AM:

To further explain the importance of understanding the meaning of a name, and especially the Name of God, let me take you to a very familiar story in the bible from the Book of Exodus.

Moses is in the backside of the wilderness of Midian watching his father-in-law's sheep, having been exiled from Egypt for forty years. As he is minding his own business, suddenly he encounters a sight that would radically change his life and destiny; a burning bush that is not consumed by the flames. As he turns to take a closer look at this unusual phenomenon, God speaks to him from the burning bush, and basically tells him to go back to the land of Egypt and tell Pharaoh to let God's people, Israel, go free.

Exodus 3:9 & 10: *"Now therefore, behold, the cry of the children of Israel is come unto me: and I have also seen the oppression wherewith the Egyptians oppress them.*
Come now therefore, and I will send thee unto Pharaoh, that thou mayest bring forth my people the children of Israel out of Egypt."

Moses protests against God and gives a whole series of excuses why he was the wrong man for the assignment. However, after those protests and excuses fell short, Moses availed himself for the assignment but not before he received an answer to a very interesting question from the One who was speaking to him from the burning bush.

Ex. 3:13: *"And Moses said unto God, Behold, when I come unto the children of Israel, and shall say unto them, The God of your* *fathers hath sent me unto you; and they shall say to me,* **What is his name?** *What shall I say unto them?"* (Emphasis mine)

The question I have here is, what has the assignment of going to deliver the children of Israel from bondage got to do with knowing the 'name' of the One sending you? What was the motive behind this unusual question?

To get to the bottom of this very important request from Moses to God, we need to understand the historical background of the one posing the question. Remember that Moses was raised in the Palaces of the greatest Monarch in his era in Egypt, which was the greatest Empire at that time. Moses, even though he was a Jew, was schooled in the traditions, customs, and religions of Egypt. He was being prepared to take over as the Pharaoh one day. Furthermore, the Israelites being slaves for over four hundred years and living in a paganism culture, had slowly but surely become assimilated into the only system they knew. Regardless of these circumstances, there were still many who held true to their belief in the God of Abraham, Isaac, and Jacob; and still believed that He would send a deliverer one day to deliver them from their oppressors.

Moses probably asked the question because he understood perfectly well that the Egyptians served many different gods. In fact, let me parenthetically insert here that the ten plagues that God sent upon Egypt by the hand of Moses, represented ten different judgments upon the different gods that were held in high regard and worshipped by the Pharaoh and the people of Egypt. Each god had his own name based on what he was able to do for the worshipper. For example, if a worshipper needed to be fertile in child bearing, she would sacrifice to the god of fertility, and not to the god of healing and vice-versa. Hence to know the name of a god was important, because it also revealed what he was CAPABLE of accomplishing for the needy worshipper. So when Moses asked God "what is your Name", he was invariably saying to God that when he went back to Egypt to tell the Jews that their God had finally heard their cry and was prepared to deliver them; he could substantiate the resume of the messenger. The people required an assurance from Moses that God was capable of doing for them what he said.

God's response to Moses must have shocked him, because he must have been expecting a specific name or title from God. Instead, God responded, "I AM THAT I AM".

Ex. 3:14 – 15: *"And God said unto Moses, I AM THAT I AM: and he said, Thus shalt thou say unto the children of Israel, I AM hath sent me unto you. And God said moreover unto Moses, Thus shalt thou say unto the children of Israel, The LORD God of your fathers, the God of Abraham, the God of Isaac, and the God of Jacob, hath sent me unto you: this is my name for ever, and this is my memorial unto all generations."*

This rendition of God's Name in Hebrew is what became known as "Yahweh" or "Jehovah" since they could not pronounce the actual meaning "YHWH". It means "to become" or "self-exist". Hence what God was telling Moses is **"I will be what I need to be when I am needed to be that"**.

In other words, God was telling Moses not to put Him in the same box or context that the Egyptians put their numerous gods. Israel's God was unlike the Egyptian gods. While they needed several different gods to solve (if they could) their multiple problems, Israel needed ONLY ONE God to solve ALL their problems. The Egyptian's gods were limited in reach and power, but Israel's God was unlimited in His reach, scope, and power. That is why later in the "exodus" of the Jews from Egyptian captivity God gave His people what is known as the "Shena"; the most important declaration in the TORAH for them to forever remember who their God was.

Deuteronomy 6:4 -5: *"Hear, O Israel:* ***The LORD our God is one LORD****: And thou shalt love the LORD thy God with all thine heart, and with all thy soul, and with all thy might."* (Emphasis mine)

This wonderful response from God is what gave Moses the confidence and trust he needed to overcome every obstacle in his path to fulfilling God's purpose for his life. Since that "burning bush" encounter with Moses and even before then, God progressively had revealed His nature, character, attributes, and power through specific encounters with His people; and gave them specific names about Himself based on that encounter which met a specific need. For example, He revealed Himself to Abraham at Mount Moriah as "Jehovah-Jireh" (Gen. 22:14), the God who sees or provides. When the children of Israel were in the Wilderness,

He revealed Himself as "Jehovah-Repheka" (Ex. 15:26), the God who heals. He is "Jehovah-Rohi" (Psalm 23:1), the Lord our Shepherd. Jehovah-Nissi (Ex. 17:15), the Lord our Conqueror and Banner of victory; Jehovah-Shalom (Judges 6:24), the Lord our Peace; Jehovah-Shamah (Ez. 48:35), the Lord who is always there. (For further study about the Revelatory Names of God, please refer to Lester Sumrall's book, *"The Names of God"*, published by Whitaker House).

> God is unlimited in His reach, scope, and power.

Throughout the bible, God has sought to reveal His nature, personality, and attributes to His creation through His various names and Titles. No one clearly demonstrated this notion than our Savior, Jesus, whose personal and eternal agenda on earth was to reveal the Father. He is the visible likeness of the invisible God, and declared to His disciples, "If you see me, then you have seen my Father also." His stated mission was to "declare the Name" of the Father.

John 17:6: *"I have **manifested thy name** unto the men which thou gavest me out of the world: thine they were, and thou gavest them me; and they have kept thy word."* (Emphasis mine)

John 17:26: *"And I have **declared unto them thy name**, and will declare it: that the love wherewith thou hast loved me may be in them, and I in them."* (Emphasis mine)

By manifesting and declaring the Name of the Father, Jesus is saying He has unveiled or made known the nature, character, and attributes of God. Hence, when He tells His disciples to hallow the Father's Name, He is telling us to acknowledge, declare, reverence, and trust in God's attributes and character which are clearly revealed, not only in His Revelatory Names, but also in the life and character of Jesus Himself. When we take time to truly "hallow His Name", we become connected to His personality which automatically generates faith to receive what His "Name" produces. We will understand what Proverbs 18:10 really means.

Prov. 18:10: *"The name of the LORD is a strong tower: the righteous runneth into it, and is safe."*

Simply put, the name of God is not only who He is, but is also what He can and will do for His child who hallows that name.

LET US PRAY:

Heavenly Father, I thank you for revealing to me that your Name is more than an identifying feature of yourself, but it is ALL you ARE and ALL you DO. Help me to hallow your Name not only in my prayers, but in my life so I don't take your Name in vain. I thank you that as I continue to discover the riches of Your Name, I'm transformed into the image of Your dear Son as I receive ALL the benefits that Your Name brings into my life. I confess today that You are my Jehovah Jireh, my Provider; Jehovah Shalom, my Peace; Jehovah Rohi, my Shepherd; Jehovah Rapha, my Healer; and Jehovah Tsikenu, my Righteousness. I will manifest Your Name to everyone around me as You manifest it to me. In Jesus Name I pray, amen!

CHAPTER 3

Prayer of Intercession

(Connecting with Divine Partnership)

Thy Kingdom come… (Luke 11:2c)

After spending some time acknowledging and adoring the Person of the Father and all His attributes, Jesus continued His teaching on prayer by asking his disciples to intercede for the Kingdom of God to be established here on earth. This is I believe the most important work given to the believer… the work of intercession. It is also the greatest privilege we can assume as we are invited by the God of the Universe to partner with Him in advancing His agenda and Kingdom here on earth. God made it crystal clear that He is looking for a man, an intercessor, who would partner with Him.

Ez. 22:30*: "And I sought for a man among them that should make up the hedge, and stand in the gap before me for the land, that I should not destroy it: but I found none."*

Who is an Intercessor?

An intercessor is one who mediates between God and man. For a long time my understanding of such a mediator or intercessor was of one who only pleaded to God on behalf of man. However, there is another dimension that an intercessor operates on. A true intercessor does not only plead on behalf of man to God, but also must be ready to plead on God's behalf to man. Intercession therefore is a two-way street. That is, the intercessor is a go-between; responsible for taking the people's case before God, and also taking God's case and cause before the people. He or she needs to know how to speak on the people's behalf (prayer) and also know how to speak on God's behalf (Prophetic utterance).

One of the most poignant examples of true intercession we witness in the bible is when Abraham stood in the gap on behalf of the cities of Sodom and Gomorrah. What we learn from this episode of intercession is that God Himself is the One who initiated the dialogue between Himself and Abraham, giving Abraham the position of partnership. God refused to take any action against these sinful cities without first consulting with His "friend" Abraham.

Gen 18: 16- 22: *And the men rose up from thence, and looked toward Sodom: and Abraham went with them to bring them on the way. And the LORD said,* **Shall I hide from Abraham that thing which I do***; Seeing that Abraham shall surely become a great and mighty nation, and all the nations of the earth shall be blessed in him? For I know him, that he will command his children and his household after him, and they shall keep the way of the LORD, to do justice and judgment; that the LORD may bring upon Abraham that which he hath spoken of him. And the LORD said, Because the cry of Sodom and Gomorrah is great, and because their sin is very grievous; I will go down now, and see whether they have done altogether according to the cry of it, which is come unto me; and if not, I will know. And the men turned their faces from thence, and went toward Sodom:* **but Abraham stood yet before the LORD.** (Emphasis mine)

Through Abraham's supplication and intercession, Lot and his family were spared God's wrath even though the city was destroyed. Even though Abraham had convinced God to spare the whole city if there were righteous people in the city, He could not even find ten. Abraham, though, through this exchange with God showed us how God values and needs our partnership in intercession to fulfill His divine purposes on the earth.

Moses was another one of God's great intercessors. One moment you see him pleading to God on the behalf of the stubborn Israelites, and the next moment you witness him pleading to the people on the behalf of God.

What made Elijah's prophetic ministry so unique and powerful was not necessarily because of his prophecies, but rather his prayers and intercession. In fact one of the few times he is mentioned in the New Testament, it was because of the power of his prayers, not because of his prophecies.

James 5:17 – 18: *"Elias was a man subject to like passions as we are, and* **he prayed earnestly** *that it might not rain: and it rained not on the earth by the space of three years and six months. And* **he prayed again**, *and the heaven gave rain, and the earth brought forth her fruit."* (Emphasis mine)

Elijah knew how to plead to God on behalf of the people and nation, but he also never shied away from pleading God's case before the people like he did on Mount Carmel. (1 Kings 18:19-21).

The ultimate example of an intercessor is Jesus Christ Himself. He is the perfect go-between, both while He was on earth and even more so now as He is seated at the right hand of God the Father. He ever lives to make intercession for the saints, according to Heb. 6; but He also does not cease to plead with man through the Holy Spirit on behalf of God.

The spirit of true intercession is the combination of the priestly anointing or office and the prophetic anointing. The former is responsible for taking the people's cause and sin before God (and also teaching them the ways of God), while the latter is responsible for taking God's case or cause (whether favorable or unfavorable) to the people.

God is calling ALL His ministers to a life of intercession. That is what Paul meant in his epistle to the Romans when he said we have been called to a ministry of reconciliation.

2 Cor. 5:18 – 20: *"And all things are of God, who hath reconciled us to himself by Jesus Christ, and hath given to us* **the ministry of reconciliation***; To wit, that God was in Christ, reconciling the world unto himself, not imputing their trespasses unto them; and hath committed unto us the* **word of reconciliation***. Now then we are ambassadors for Christ, as though God did beseech you by us:*

*we pray you in Christ's stead, **be ye reconciled to God.**"* (Emphasis mine)

Misconceptions of Intercession:

There are many in the Body of Christ who either consciously or unconsciously neglect or dismiss (out rightly) the importance of prayer/intercession in the process of reconciling men to God, and restoring the Kingdom of God on earth. Those who tend to dismiss it often claim that since God is sovereign, He does not need man's intervention to do anything. Hence their predisposition is: 'God will do what He wants to do,

> *God is calling ALL His ministers to a life of intercession.*

where He wants to do it, when He wants to do it, how He wants to do it, and with whom or to whom He wants to do it'. As it concerns the work of salvation, they claim God's sovereignty has already predestinated those that would be saved, and hence what anyone does or does not do would not have any effect on what has already been predestinated in His sovereignty.

This school of thought obviously does not pass true biblical interpretation of God's character and sovereignty. Indeed, God is

Sovereign and hence can do what He chooses to do, when He chooses to do so, and how He chooses to do so. That is the very reason why God in His sovereignty chose to give man authority and dominion in the earth realm to execute His will and purpose. In other words, He gave man a seat at the table, if you will, in deciding the outcomes of the events on earth. Therefore, without man's partnership through intercession, as John Wesley aptly put it, it seems like God's hands are tied behind him for Him to accomplish what He would want to accomplish on earth. That is why He declared unequivocally in Ez. 22:30 that He was looking for a man to stand in the gap. We will discuss this thought further later in this chapter.

> *God has chosen in His sovereignty, not to do anything without our partnership.*

Those who do not out-rightly dismiss the need and role of intercession, but nonetheless ignore or neglect its use and power most often put more focus or emphasis on the other important aspects of reconciliation such as preaching (Evangelism to non-believers and prophetic utterance to believers). Jesus' lifestyle in ministry on earth should debunk such attitudes.

As we already discussed, prayer and intercession were at the core of His life and ministry. Not only did He demonstrate it, but it was one of His favorite topics to teach on. He taught on prayer (intercession) more than evangelism or preaching. One day Jesus gave His disciples an assignment that must have blown their minds away. Jesus basically made a direct correlation between the number of laborers in the field of evangelism and prayer.

Luke 10:2: *"Therefore said he unto them, The harvest truly is great, but the labourers are few:* **pray ye therefore the Lord of the harvest***, that he would send forth labourers into his harvest."* (Emphasis mine)

Why would a sovereign God need our prayers to send laborers into His harvest? Is not God capable by Himself to win the whole world to Himself without the help of any human agency? Of course He can, but as we iterated earlier, He has chosen in His sovereignty not to do anything without our partnership. What an amazing thought, that even in the most important work of all in dealing with the eternal souls of humans that the Father requires our partnership and participation through intercession to release more laborers into His field, thus resulting in the greatest harvest of souls we have ever witnessed. This should make the most ardent Evangelist amongst us to shout for joy, while simultaneously kneeling down to pray for more laborers.

Thy Kingdom Come:

God's plan has always been that His Church or Eklesia, His called out ones, will enforce the boundaries of the kingdom of God now, and in the millennial reign of Jesus actually take over the kingdoms of this world.

Luke 19:13: *"And he called his ten servants, and delivered them ten pounds, and said onto them,* **occupy till I come***"* (Emphasis mine)

Rev. 11:15: *"And the seventh angel sounded; and there were great voices in heaven, saying,* **The kingdoms of this world are become the kingdoms of our Lord, and of his Christ***; and he shall reign for ever and ever"* (Emphasis mine)

In the beginning, God gave Adam dominion over the whole earth in the Garden of Eden (Gen. 1:26), and as a result of sin, Adam gave or transferred that dominion into the hands of the devil (Gen. 3). Ever since then (until Christ) the devil has had legal rule over the kingdoms of this world and hence has freely perpetuated his own evil devices in the world as we can see just by watching the evening news.

When Adam handed over the keys of authority to Satan through the beguiling of Eve, and his willing participation, the devil turned Kosmos (World systems) into chaos; causing sin, disease, depravity, and death to reign instead of God's Kingdom of righteousness, peace, and joy in the Holy Ghost (Romans 14:17).

Eph. 2:2: *"Wherein in time past ye walked according to the course of this world, according to the prince of the power of the air, the spirit that now worketh in the children of disobedience."*

1 John 5:19: *"And we know that we are of God, and the whole world lieth in wickedness."*

As a direct result of the fall, Satan has successfully deceived many of Adam's descendants into worshiping or aligning themselves with his ways in order to give them power, fame and/or fortune. It is the reason why he asked Jesus on the "mount of temptation" to worship him so that he would give him the kingdoms of this world and all its glory, which were delivered unto him. (Luke 4:6 & Matt. 4:8)

Luke 4:5 & 6: *"And the devil, taking him up into an high mountain, shewed unto him all the kingdoms of the world in a moment of time. And the devil said unto him, All this power will I give thee, and the glory of them: for that is delivered unto me; and to whomsoever I will I give it."*

We have to recognize that up until this period, the devil indeed had it to give. That is why the Lord did not argue with him and tell him he was lying but simply resisted him with the word of God. Jesus understood the transfer that took place in Eden and knew that He was appointed to die to retrieve back for man what he freely and willingly gave away. He knew His time was coming when the kingdoms of the world were going to be restored back to God through his Church.

And so we fast forward past three years of signs and wonders by Jesus Christ, who did not contaminate Himself with anything from the world or the devil, to his death and resurrection. When He resurrected from the dead, He stripped the devil of ALL his authority and restored the keys of the kingdom to us. He said ALL power has been given to me in heaven and earth, therefore go into all the **world** or **nations** (Greek - Kosmos & ethnos) and make disciples by preaching the gospel of the kingdom. (Matt. 28:18 & 19; Luke 4:6 - paraphrase)

When Jesus said to go into ALL the world or Nations, He was not just referring to geographical or demographical locations as many in the church have believed and still believe and teach. The word "nations" in the Matthew account is the Greek word "ethnos" which translates ethnicities or ethnic groups. In the Mark account, the word "world" is the Greek word "Kosmos" which means "the sum total of the material universe, the beauty in it, and the sum total of persons living in the world". It refers to the systems that exist in the world and that make it habitable.

What Jesus was saying to us was for us to infiltrate the cultures of this world or to infiltrate ALL the strata of society that exists in the world with the gospel of the Kingdom. These strata of society are what, I believe, for the most part is referred to as the "Kingdoms of this World" which have now become the Kingdoms of our Lord and of his Christ which is the Church. According to 2 Chron. 36 , He has given these kingdoms to us (the church) and charged us to build Him a house or establish His Kingdom or

Lordship in the world, stripping the devil of his illegitimate right and hold on it.

God spoke to Abraham in Rom. 4:13 and told him that he was going to be "the heir of the world". We have to realize that even though the promise was made to Abraham, our forefather through faith in Christ Jesus, he did not actually obtain it (Heb. 11). He was just an heir, and since he still lived under the old covenant there was no way he could actually fully appropriate that promise because the world was still under the legal control of the devil. Not until the death and resurrection of our Lord, Savior and also senior brother Jesus Christ, was that promise able to be appropriated and made effective. We have been made heirs together with Christ and hence heirs of this world through faith and actuality. What Abraham could not actually possess, we now possess through Jesus Christ. We now possess the keys of the kingdom and we have been called to restore the kingdoms of this world to the rule of the resurrected Lord of Glory.

Matt. 16:19: *"And I will give unto thee the keys of the kingdom of heaven: and whatsoever thou shalt bind on earth shall be bound in* *heaven: and whatsoever thou shalt loose on earth shall be loosed in heaven."*

In order to effectively accomplish the task of restoring the kingdoms of this world to God, we need to know what those kingdoms are. There are at least seven (7) strata of our society or world which represent the kingdoms of this world. As we shall see, each kingdom is under the influence of the adversary who seeks to dominate them by either keeping the church away from them by deceit, or stripping us of the authority that we already have over them.

We need to remember that the devil was stripped of his legal right and control over these kingdoms through the death and resurrection of Jesus, but he still wields strong influence and control by permission through human agency over all or some of these areas. It is up to the Church to rise up in partnership with God through the power of intercession and evangelism to pursue, overtake and recover ALL that the enemy has stolen and said belongs to him. It is up to the church to obey the teaching of our

Lord in crying to God: "Let your Kingdom come, and let your will be done on Earth as it is done in Heaven."

According to www.reclaim7mountains.com, "There are 7 Mountains of Influence in Culture." The site goes onto reveal: "In 1975, Bill Bright, founder of Campus Crusade, and Loren Cunningham, founder of Youth With a Mission, had lunch together in Colorado. God simultaneously gave each of these change agents a message to give to the other. During that same time frame Francis Schaeffer was given a similar message. That message was that if we are to impact any nation for Jesus Christ, then we would have to affect the seven spheres, or mountains of society that are the pillars of any society. These seven mountains are business, government, media, arts and entertainment, education, the family and religion. There are many subgroups under these main categories. About a month later the Lord showed Francis Schaeffer the same thing. In essence, God was telling these three change agents where the battlefield was."

Through prayer, intercession, and strategic evangelism, God has mandated His Church to infiltrate and subdue these strata of society to reflect His character and values.

Family:

The God ordained institution of family is under fire and attack! Same sex marriage, civil unions, divorce and such are on the rise to undermine the God established and time-honored institution of marriage.

Through intercession we can take our families back and restore marriage as God intended for it to be. Husbands will be empowered to love, cherish and honor their wives; while wives will be empowered to submit and honor their husbands. Our children will be taught in the ways of God, to honor authority and obey their parents.

Above all, our intercession will restore fatherhood in our neighborhoods and broken society, empowering fathers to be good fathers; providing, protecting and raising their children in the fear and admonition of the Lord, and making their homes houses of prayer. Our intercession will restore the true essence of motherhood to mothers (working or stay-at-home) to nurture and cover their homes with love, peace and joy. Let us contend in prayer and intercession for the institution of the family as it forms the pillars upon which the church and the nation (USA) are built upon. (Eph. 5:22-33; 6:1-4)

True Religion:

True religion is under siege as false religions like Islam and the occult (including the New Age Movement) continue to rise and seemingly take over nations. The Church of the Lord Jesus Christ, the greatest force for good in the earth, seems to be satisfied to stay in our 'sanctuaries' and just play church. The church in so many ways and places has become like a giant lulled to sleep with apathy and self indulgence. At the same time, the people of the world continue to grapple in darkness seeking for real power, love and peace which can be found only through a dynamic relationship with our Lord and Savior Jesus Christ. Through intercession, God will cause the Church to arise in power, glory, and demonstration;

showing the world and other false religions that there is no power but the power of Christ. The world must know that there is no name given among men in heaven or on earth or under the earth where mankind has an opportunity to be saved, except by the name of Jesus. We need to partner with God in intercession so that His Word concerning the Church will be accomplished.

Is. 2:2: *"And it shall come to pass in the last days, that the mountain of the LORD'S house shall be established in the top of the mountains, and shall be exalted above the hills; and all nations shall flow unto it."*

Even though this scripture in context refers to what will happen when Jesus bursts through the eastern sky in His second coming; destroying His adversaries and establishing His throne in Jerusalem; it also applies to God's intention for His Church now. He intends for His Church to be exalted above every other religion and for the nations of the world to be influenced by 'her'. The way God intends for His Kingdom to truly come on earth is for His Church to be restored back to its original purpose, as a House of Prayer for all nations.

Is. 56:7: *"Even them will I bring to my holy mountain, and make them joyful in my house of prayer: their burnt offerings and their sacrifices shall be accepted upon mine altar; for mine house shall be called an house of prayer for all people."*

Matt. 21:13: *"And said unto them, It is written, My house shall be called the house of prayer; but ye have made it a den of thieves."*

The church was birthed in prayer and power; and the only way she is going to continue to be powerful and relevant in these last days is for her to return to her place of prayer, intercession, and intimacy with her Bridegroom. We need to realize that the only reason Adam had dominion on earth was due to His unrestrained communion

> *Adam had dominion on earth due to His unrestrained communion with God.*

with God. The day he lost his dominion was the day he refused, because of sin, to commune with God. You and I as the church or the Body of Christ will begin once again to walk in our God ordained authority and power the moment we choose to become intimate intercessors before God.

It is time to arise and shine, for we recognize that our light, fire or power has come and the glory of the Lord is risen upon us (Is. 60:1). It is time to restore Pentecost through intercession in the church of the Lord Jesus Christ.

Government/Politics:

We, the Church, have been lied to by the devil and religious traditional leaders for so long; telling us that we did not belong in the political arena. Hence we have been satisfied to stay in our sanctuaries and just 'prayed' and cursed the darkness around us while we buried our light under a bushel in the 'safety' of our sanctuaries. We have allowed the saying "politics is dirty" to prevent us from going in. Our prayers were done in the format of criticism or complaints to God concerning how horrible our political leaders are. Therefore, by default, we have allowed the ungodly to bear rule over us. Well, if politics is dirty, who better to clean it up but the saints of God? We have to remember that all authority (including political or governmental) is ordained and established by God and for God.

Rom. 13:1: *"Let every soul be subject unto the higher powers. For there is no power but of God: the powers that be are ordained of God."*

The bible also makes it clear in Prov. 29:2 that "when the righteous are in power or authority, the people rejoice; but when the wicked bear rule, the people moan". As in Old Testament times, it is necessary and beneficial for there to be a righteous King or President (one who does what is right before God) in a nation for there to be an authentic, sustained culture shaking and transforming revival.

Even though there was a powerful manifestation of God's power during Elijah's time, the spiritual awakening that resulted from his victorious confrontation with the prophets of Baal was not long lived as long as Ahab and Jezebel were still in the Castle as King and Queen. However, the strongest and the most long lasting spiritual awakening and revival in the history of the Kings of Israel and Judah occurred during the reign of Josiah. The account of the reign of King Josiah in 2 Kings 21 and 22, should become the blueprint for us the people of God, especially those called to governmental leadership, to restore our nation(s) from paths of injustice, immorality, and ruin to that of moral clarity, justice, and prosperity. As you read about the life of Josiah, you will learn about what he did to restore the House of God, the law of God, and the favor of God over His people.

We are to strongly intercede for God to raise up leaders like Josiah who fear the Lord and desire to do what is right in the sight of the Lord.

2 Kings 22:1 & 2: *"Josiah was eight years old when he began to reign, and he reigned thirty and one years in Jerusalem. And his mother's name was Jedidah, the daughter of Adaiah of Boscath. And he did that which was right in the sight of the LORD, and walked in all the way of David his father, and turned not aside to the right hand or to the left."*

It is time to take Politics back from the ungodly and allow God to raise up the righteous in positions of leadership whether on the school board, City Council, Mayor, Senate, Congress, Judiciary, or even the Presidency. (Rom. 13:1-7, Prov. 29:3 & 1 Tim. 2:1-6)

Education:

The current structure of our educational system across the globe is mostly under the influence of the evil one. I believe without a shadow of a doubt that the primary goal of education should be to lead one ultimately to the knowledge of God. By training the spirit, soul, and body of young men and women in the knowledge of God whether in the sciences, languages, or arts; they are better equipped to attain to their fullest God ordained potential. However, the enemy has successfully corrupted our system of education to become actually anti-God.

Education, especially public education, has become more humanistic and anti everything the church stands for and believes in. Our children are being taught situational ethics, values clarification, Darwinian Theory of evolution and such like; all of which oppose God and His principles. When prayer and bible reading are banned from our public schools and Christian children are forbidden from freely expressing and witnessing their faith in the hall ways, God is also banned. No wonder that crime, violence, dishonoring of authority, and promiscuity leading to teen-age pregnancy is at an all time high with no end in sight – seemingly.

It is time for the Church to rise and take a stand in intercession for education as God intended it to be. It is time to take back and restore godly values into the schools and into the curriculum. It is time to pray for

> *Education of our children is the battleground of all ages.*

the remnant in these schools to rise and shine the light of the gospel of Jesus. It is time for revival to break forth among the youth in the high schools and colleges and restore godliness in their institutions. It is time to take education back through prayer and intercession asking God to cause His will to be done in School Board meetings, so that sound counsel would prevail in the schools. We need to intercede on behalf of the Colleges and Universities that Christian students will be bold to challenge the humanistic world view being propagated by their so called Professors, and also be able to witness their faith freely.

We need to be aware of the fact that the enemy is relentless in his efforts to capture the minds of every generation at the early stages through their education. If he cannot wipe them out while they are in the womb through abortion, then he must influence and perhaps control their destiny by what they are taught.

He is after our brightest and strongest just as he showed when he inspired King Nebuchadnezzar, after he destroyed Jerusalem, to capture some of the people to serve him in his courts. Note his main target:

Daniel 1:3 & 4: *"And the king spake unto Ashpenaz the master of his eunuchs, that he should bring certain of the children of Israel, and of the king's seed, and of the princes;*
*Children in whom was **no blemish, but well favored, and skilful in all wisdom, and cunning in knowledge, and understanding science**, and such as had ability in them to stand in the king's palace, and whom they might teach the learning and the tongue of the Chaldeans."* (Emphasis mine)

Education of our children is the battleground of all ages, because the devil knows that if he can capture and corrupt the minds of the young men and women just as he tried to do with Daniel and his friends, he would be successful in controlling not just them, but those who would come after them since they will become the fathers, mothers, and leaders of the next generation… and before you know it three or four generations later, the whole nation is swept in his diabolical lies. If anyone doubts this satanic inspired process, all they have to do is look at the greatest nation on earth, the United States of America; a nation built on Judeo-Christian values but now looks in many parts and ways like Sodom and Gomorrah. What happened?

While the Church slept, the enemy crept in and started perpetrating his agenda in the schools, especially in the colleges to the extent that even Christian colleges like Harvard University became swept up in the lies of the enemy, and have now actually become the epicenters of the propagation of his diabolical agenda. What used to be anathema in the 1940's and 1950's like abortion and homosexual lifestyle, to name just a couple, are now not only openly accepted in our general society, but is actually being taught in the elementary schools as general norm.

The church has to wake up from her slumber and engage the enemy and his educational agenda through intercession. We need to pray that God would strengthen and sustain young men and women, like Daniel and his three friends, who would refuse to take the bait of the devil and purpose to keep themselves pure before the Lord.

Dan. 1:8: *"But Daniel purposed in his heart that he would not defile himself with the portion of the king's meat, nor with the wine which he drank: therefore he requested of the prince of the eunuchs that he might not defile himself."*

Business/Commerce:

It is time to take the business (economics and commerce sectors) back from the powers of darkness. Most of the church has been lied to for many generations by the devil and religious traditions. The lie is this: poverty is equal to or consistent with piety. That is a deception that has been so much perpetuated in the house of God that even though many desire and confess that they are blessed or going to be blessed by God, they do not actually believe it. And even if they do, their expectation of such a blessing so much falls below what God actually wants to do for them.

Through the power of intercession, we have to break the spirit of poverty and replace the poverty mentality with a Kingdom mentality which claims ALL the benefits of redemption, including financial prosperity. God wants to bless his people so that they would become a blessing like Abraham was and Joseph too. To do that, we have to realize that the blessing is not going to just fall from the skies because we pray, scream or spin around seven times. God said He has given us the power to get wealth. This means He expects us through our covenant with Him, confirmed through biblical tithing and seed sowing, to get into the business world and possess it. Jesus said, "Occupy till I come", which being translated from the original Greek would read, "do business till I come". It is high time for the Church to stop waiting to be blessed but become a blessing by allowing God to empower us with faith, wisdom and creative ideas that, like Joseph, we become distribution centers. (Deut. 8:18; 28:1-14 & 3 John: 2)

Media:

The bible calls the devil "the Prince of the power of the air" (Eph. 2:2). It seems that the devil has cunningly succeeded in turning the media into his own diabolical tool to perpetrate his evil in our world today. Through the TV, internet, radio, and even video games, he has succeeded in holding people captive at his will. Many homes have been ravaged by divorce because men can't keep their eyes from pornographic images on their TV and computer screens; our children are being captivated by violent and explicit sexual messages through their video games; and most of all the media which we are supposed to trust to inform the public, is now become "public enemy #1" spawning lies and deceit to influence the culture negatively.

We have to agree that the media is not bad in itself, but rather how it is used is what corrupts. God is the originator of everything good, and the media is a good thing created by God for his own pleasure. But unless the church arise and possess through prayer and intercession this stratum of society from the hands of the "prince of the air", our societies are going to continue to degenerate without remedy as the enemy spawns his lies through the media. It is time to restore the media to the Prince of Peace and use it to propagate the gospel of the Lord Jesus Christ.

Entertainment:

I believe that entertainment is an area God is desperately calling the Church to take back and take over through intercession. I even believe that we have started making inroads with the great accomplishments being achieved by many Christian artists. There are now more Christian movies in Hollywood than ever before. These movies don't only stay in America, but they go all over the world with subtitles so that people can be ministered to while being entertained.

It is vital that the Christians become even more involved in this medium because everyone loves entertainment. We refer to movie stars and sports personalities as celebrities or icons. They don't know or understand how to return the glory to God for the influence they hold over so many people; instead they flaunt their fame and fortune with gross ungodly actions. Our youth lusts for their status and seek to portray or reproduce what they have seen. Sadly, the youth are not the only ones who want what these celebrities have; it seem as though our pastors have gotten hungry for their own celebrity status and they desire the quickest and surest way to fame, fortune and glory!

The devil has successfully deceived many, like he tried with Jesus on the 'mount of temptation', into bowing to him in order to receive fame and fortune only to realize that all that glittered was not gold. Shattered lives and broken dreams are the result of such a partnership, but many still have not learned. True fame and fortune comes from God, and when He gives it no man or devil can take it away. He told Abraham He would make him rich and famous (Gen. 12:2) and He did, and after 4,000 years he still is. He told Solomon He would make him rich and famous (1 Kings 3:11-14), and today he still is considered the richest man who has ever lived. The Bible says Jesus came out from the wilderness, after withstanding the devil for forty days, with power and His fame went out before Him. If you want fame and fortune, God has it and is willing to give it to those He chooses. The Bible says, "But seek ye first the Kingdom of God and His righteousness; and all these things…" (fame and fortune) which the heathen seek, "shall be added unto you." (Matt. 6:33)

Since entertainment is a part of our society and reaches out to everyone, the Church has to possess it and restore it to God, using it to establish His Kingdom and bringing glory to His name.

Through the power of intercession, we can restore the kingdoms of this world to become "the Kingdoms of our God and His Christ".

LET US PRAY:

Father, I thank you for revealing your purpose for my life here on earth; to be a partner with you as you establish your Kingdom here on earth. Forgive me for the times when I have not responded to the call of partnership through intercession. I ask you to continue to open my eyes of understanding concerning these things and baptize me afresh with the spirit of prayer and intercession. Give me a fresh burden to stand before you in prayer to intercede for the business, government, media, arts and entertainment, education, family and religion spheres of influence in my city and nation. Father I pray; "let your Kingdom come". Amen!

CHAPTER 4

Prayer of Agreement
(Connecting to Divine Purpose)

Thy will be done, as in heaven, so in earth. (Luke 11:2d)

Closely related to the prayer of intercession is the prayer of agreement. God's ultimate desire, purpose, and will is that what takes place in Heaven will simultaneously take place on Earth. In other words, Earth is supposed to be a reflection of Heaven.

From the creation, God intended for Earth to become a physical extension of Heaven. While He governed and ruled in Heaven, man (Adam) was to rule and govern on earth as God's representative. The way man was to effectively do this was to maintain a constant communion with God, and reproduce what he saw in Heaven on Earth. Of course, Satan and sin disrupted God's original plan when man chose to partner with the Devil and partake of the forbidden fruit in the midst of the garden. However, God never gave up on His original plan. Earth will become a reflection of Heaven!

If God's will on Earth is supposed to reflect His will in Heaven, then it is imperative for us to know what that will is. We therefore don't pray this prayer from a stand point of ignorance of what His will is. In fact the effectiveness and strength of this prayer comes from the fact that we know what His will is; and in agreement with Him, we ask Him to enforce that will. In essence, we ask God in prayer to duplicate what we see taking place in Heaven, and place that same thing on the Earth. Many people in the Church agree in principle to this assertion; however I believe there is a little bit of a misunderstanding about the full extent of what Jesus meant by "Thy will be done on earth as it is in heaven".

Many explain God's will in heaven in terms of what does not take place there, rather than what actually takes place there. They assert, rightly so, that since there is no sickness, poverty, disease, and any other vice in Heaven; that is the will God also wants to enforce on Earth. Therefore, when we pray "Thy will be done on earth as it is in Heaven" we are asking God to eradicate the injustices caused by all these vices we witness day to day on Earth. As much as this explanation is valid, I believe it does not do justice to what Jesus intended for us through this powerful lesson on prayer.

This prayer of agreement is more about praying for what we see happening in Heaven to happen on Earth. If this is true, then it is important to know exactly what is currently taking place in Heaven, so we can agree with God to reproduce it here on earth.

Rev. 4:1-11: *"After this I looked, and, behold, a door was opened in heaven: and the first voice which I heard was as it were of a trumpet talking with me; which said, Come up hither, and I will shew thee things which must be hereafter. And immediately I was in the spirit: and, behold, a throne was set in heaven, and one sat on the throne. And he that sat was to look upon like a jasper and a sardine stone: and there was a rainbow round about the throne, in sight like unto an emerald. And round about the throne were four and twenty seats: and upon the seats I saw four and twenty elders sitting, clothed in white raiment; and they had on their heads crowns of gold. And out of the throne proceeded lightnings and thunderings and voices: and there were seven lamps of fire burning before the throne, which are the seven Spirits of God. And before the throne there was a sea of glass like unto crystal: and in the midst of the throne, and round about the throne, were four beasts full of eyes before and behind. And the first beast was like a lion, and the second beast like a calf, and the third beast had a face as a man, and the fourth beast was like a flying eagle. And the four beasts had each of them six wings about him; and they were full of eyes within: and* **they rest not day and night**, *saying, Holy, holy, holy, Lord God Almighty, which was, and is, and is to come.*

And when those beasts give glory and honour and thanks to him that sat on the throne, who liveth for ever and ever, The four and twenty elders fall down before him that sat on the throne, and worship him that liveth for ever and ever, and cast their crowns before the throne, saying, Thou art worthy, O Lord, to receive glory and honour and power: for thou hast created all things, and for thy pleasure they are and were created." (Emphasis mine)

As you can see, around the Throne of God the four living creatures and the twenty four elders gaze on the Beauty of the One who sits on the throne day and night. The description of these creatures is intriguing in that they have eyes everywhere. These eyes constantly gaze on the splendor of the beauty of God. And as they view the transcendent Holiness of God, they are awestruck and can't help but to exclaim, "Holy.

> **Earth is supposed to be a reflection of Heaven.**

Holy, Holy ..." This is similar to the experience Isaiah had when he encountered the majesty of God in the temple in Isaiah 6.

Is. 6:1-4: *"In the year that king Uzziah died I saw also the Lord sitting upon a throne, high and lifted up, and his train filled the temple. Above it stood the seraphims: each one had six wings; with twain he covered his face, and with twain he covered his feet, and with twain he did fly. And one cried unto another, and said, Holy, holy, holy, is the LORD of hosts: the whole earth is full of his glory. And the posts of the door moved at the voice of him that cried, and the house was filled with smoke."*

God's will has always been that Earth will have a day and night (24/7) worship and prayer culture just as we see in Heaven. God prophesied through the Prophet Malachi of this intention when He said in Malachi 1:11:

Malachi 1:11: *"For from the rising of the sun even unto the going down of the same my name shall be great among the Gentiles; and in **every place incense shall be offered unto my name**, and a pure offering: for my name shall be great among the heathen, saith the LORD of hosts."* (Emphasis mine)

This is God's will for Earth, that from the rising of the sun (day) to the going down of the same (night), incense (worship and prayer) will be offered unto His Name, so that His Name will be great and magnified

> *God chooses to govern in an atmosphere of unceasing prayer and worship.*

in the earth. We see this theme of God throughout scripture. Why is this so important to God? It is because when He opens our eyes to see a glimpse of Heaven, what we see is a glorious view of unceasing prayer, worship, and adoration around the Throne of God. In the very Temple of God in Heaven where His Throne is located, there are Angels worshipping constantly without ceasing.

It is very important to note that God chooses to govern in an atmosphere of unceasing prayer and worship. His judgments and blessings are only released through the agency and atmosphere of prayer and worship. God in essence will do nothing except in answer to prayer and worship.

The Exodus

After Adam and Eve rebelled against God and therefore ceded control and authority of the earth to the devil, God's original plan and will that earth will be a reflection of heaven was temporarily disrupted. Throughout the ensuing generations, from Seth, Enoch, Noah, all the way to Abraham, God began to reveal and restore His original intention for man. He proved through these men that man's primary responsibility on the earth was to subdue it through an intimate relationship with Him. These men are known more for their faith; but what many do not realize is that it was their prayer life and communion with God that fueled their faith and commended them to God.

Gen. 4:26: *"And to Seth, to him also there was born a son; and he called his name Enos:* ***then began men to call upon the name of the LORD"*** (Emphasis mine)

However, the greatest place we see God really begin to restore His will of continuous prayer and worship on earth as it is in heaven is when He delivered His people Israel from Egyptian captivity. What was the primary reason for their deliverance? Before you respond and say God delivered them so they would go to a land flowing with milk and honey, we need to check the scriptures again.

Ex. 5:1 & 3: *"And afterward Moses and Aaron went in, and told Pharaoh, Thus saith the LORD God of Israel, Let my people go, that they may hold a feast unto me in the wilderness. And they said, The God of the Hebrews hath met with us: let us go, we pray thee, three days' journey into the desert, and sacrifice unto the LORD our God; lest he fall upon us with pestilence, or with the sword."*

Even though Canaan, the land flowing with milk and honey, was to be their inheritance and possession, it was not their primary inheritance and goal for their deliverance. The primary goal and purpose for their deliverance from Egypt was to meet God in the Wilderness, and build Him a Tabernacle or Sanctuary where unceasing prayer and worship would ascend to heaven. Just like the Israelites, the main purpose God, through the shed blood of

Jesus, has delivered us out of sin and bondage is not to give us cars, houses, or a "better" life; but that we will first of all have an encounter with Him. Secondly, we are to become living sanctuaries creating an atmosphere on earth that reflect heaven. Just like the Jews, He wants to be our inheritance, before He gives us our secondary inheritance. Heaven is not our inheritance. God is our inheritance; and He desires more than anything that we experience heaven on earth now.

When Pharaoh finally decided to let the children of Israel depart from Egypt, their first destination was to go to the mountain of God, Mount Sinai. Once again God's purpose for teaching them some pertinent lessons before they could really possess the land was twofold:

1. He wanted them to have a personal encounter with Him:

Ex. 19:3-6, *"And Moses went up unto God, and the LORD called unto him out of the mountain, saying, Thus shalt thou say to the house of Jacob, and tell the children of Israel; Ye have seen what I did unto the Egyptians, and how I bare you on eagles' wings, and* **brought you unto myself***. Now therefore, if ye will obey my voice indeed, and keep my covenant, then ye shall be a peculiar treasure unto me above all people: for all the earth is mine: And ye shall be unto me a kingdom of priests, and an holy nation. These are the words which thou shalt speak unto the children of Israel."*

2. Build a Tabernacle on earth after the pattern of that which is in heaven:

Ex. 25:1-9 *"And the LORD spake unto Moses, saying, Speak unto the children of Israel, that they bring me an offering: of every man that giveth it willingly with his heart ye shall take my offering. And this is the offering which ye shall take of them; gold, and silver, and brass, And blue, and purple, and scarlet, and fine linen, and goats' hair, And rams' skins dyed red, and badgers' skins, and shittim wood, Oil for the light, spices for anointing oil, and for sweet incense, Onyx stones, and stones to be set in the ephod, and in the breastplate.* **And let them make me a sanctuary; that I may dwell among them. According to all that I shew thee, after the pattern of the tabernacle,** *and the pattern of all the instruments thereof, even so shall ye make it."* (Emphasis mine)

The instruction to Moses could not be clearer. In fact, God took Moses on a tour of the heavenly Tabernacle where 24/7 prayer and worship goes on around the Throne of God as described earlier in the Book of Revelation chapter four. I believe God was simply saying to Moses, 'I want you to reproduce everything you see here in heaven on earth, and just as my Presence and Glory fills and pervades everything in heaven, so shall it be also on earth'. This is God's will; to have a people who believe He is worthy of unceasing, unhindered prayer and worship.

Moses obeyed God and built the Tabernacle according to the heavenly pattern. He then put the Ark of God, which was a replica of the Throne of God with the Mercy seat and the covering Cherubs, in the Holies of Holies. God also instructed Moses to assign Priests who would minister before the Ark continuously, not allowing the fire on the Altar to ever go out day nor night.

Lev. 6:12 & 13: *"And the fire upon the altar shall be burning in it; it shall not be put out: and the priest shall burn wood on it every morning, and lay the burnt offering in order upon it; and he shall burn thereon the fat of the peace offerings.* ***The fire shall ever be burning upon the altar; it shall never go out.****"* (Emphasis mine)

The fire on the altar represented the prayers of the children of God and was supposed to be serviced day and night by the Priests who were appointed and sanctified for that particular purpose. God's intention for Moses' Tabernacle was that the people would always know that He dwelt amongst them, and as long as the Tabernacle with the Ark of Covenant was in their midst, they would never have to be afraid of their adversaries. God's plan from the very beginning of creation till now has been to dwell amongst His people if they would walk in obedience, and create an atmosphere through prayer and worship conducive for His Presence to abide.

God's plan and intention for His people then and now is that He might actually dwell in us and with us.

Ex. 25:8: *"And let them make me a sanctuary; **that I may dwell among them**."* (Emphasis mine)

2 Cor. 6:16 – 18: *"And what agreement hath the temple of God with idols? for ye are the temple of the living God; as God hath said**, I will dwell in them, and walk in them; and I will be their God, and they shall be my people**. Wherefore come out from among them, and be ye separate, saith the Lord, and touch not the unclean thing; and I will receive you, And will be a Father unto you, and ye shall be my sons and daughters, saith the Lord Almighty."* (Emphasis mine)

After Moses died and the Children of Israel entered into their promised land, we do not hear or see any active adherence to God's ordinance concerning the Tabernacle and its significance, until Shiloh where the Ark of Covenant was kept. Eli and his sons were Priests during this time. This is also where we encounter the story of the greatest Prophet in Israel's history; Samuel, who also ministered before the Presence of the Lord in Shiloh. The Prophet

Samuel's ministry began as a result of encountering God as he spent time in His Presence day and night.

1 Sam. 1:3: *"And this man [Eli] went up out of his city yearly to worship and to sacrifice unto the LORD of hosts in Shiloh. And the two sons of Eli, Hophni and Phinehas, the priests of the LORD, were there."*

1 Sam. 2:18: *"But Samuel ministered before the LORD, being a child, girded with a linen ephod."*

1 Sam. 3:3: *"And **ere the lamp of God** went out in the temple of the LORD, where the ark of God was, and Samuel was laid down to sleep."*

After the Ark was captured and subsequently returned by the Philistines; and throughout the reign of Israel's first king, Saul, we once again encounter a period where the Tabernacle and the Ark of God were not central to the lifestyle of God's people. However, since God always intends for His will in Heaven to be done on Earth, He found a willing partner in David, the man after God's own heart, to agree with Him. King David initiated the restoration of day and night prayer and worship back into the fabric of the nation and the people of God.

The Tabernacle of David

King David in Psalm 27:4 said, "One thing have I desired of the Lord, that will I seek after; that I may dwell in the house of the Lord all the days of my life, to behold the beauty of the Lord, and to enquire in his temple."

Around 1000 BC, as an outflow of his heart, David commanded that the Ark of the Covenant be brought up on the shoulders of the Levites amidst the sound of songs and musical instruments to his new capital, Jerusalem. There he had it placed in a tent and appointed 288 prophetic singers and 4,000 musicians to minister before the Lord.

1 Chronicles 16:40: *"To offer burnt offerings unto the LORD upon the altar of the burnt offering continually morning and evening, and to do according to all that is written in the law of the LORD, which he commanded Israel"*

It is worth reading the whole account of the return of the Ark of God to Jerusalem; and the purpose and significance of it from 1 Chron. 15:1 – 17:27. This was unlike anything that had been done in Israel's history, but it was God's plan for Israel.

The Davidic Order of Worship:

Although the tabernacle was replaced by a temple, the Davidic order of worship was embraced and reinstituted by seven subsequent leaders in the history of Israel and Judah. Each time this order of worship was reintroduced, spiritual breakthrough, deliverance and military victory followed.

- Solomon instructed that worship in the temple should be in accordance with the Davidic order (2 Chron. 8:14–15).
- Jehoshaphat defeated Moab and Ammon by setting singers up in accordance with the Davidic order: singers at the front of the army singing the Great Hallel. Jehoshaphat reinstituted Davidic worship in the temple (2 Chron. 20:20–22, 28).
- Joash, through the help of Jehoiada the priest, repaired the House of God and reinstituted the Davidic order of worship (2 Chron. 23:1 – 24:27).

- Hezekiah cleansed and re-consecrated the temple, and reinstituted the Davidic order of worship (2 Chron. 29:1–36; 30:21).
- Josiah reinstituted Davidic worship (2 Chron. 35:1–27).
- Ezra and Nehemiah, returning from Babylon, reinstituted Davidic worship (Ezra 3:10; Neh. 12:28–47).

According to information I found on www.ihop.org, "Historians have also speculated that around the time of Jesus, in their search to find communion with God, the Essenes of the Judean wilderness reinstituted Davidic worship as part of their life of prayer and fasting."

24/7 Prayer in the Twentieth Century:

In 1973, David Yonggi Cho, Pastor of the Yoido Full Gospel Church in Seoul, South Korea, established Prayer Mountain with night-and-day prayer. Prayer Mountain was soon attracting over a million visitors per year, as people would spend retreats in the prayer cells provided on the mountain. Cho had a commitment to continuous prayer, to faith and to establishing small discipleship cells in his church. Perhaps as a result, Cho's church rapidly expanded to become the largest church congregation on the globe, with membership now over 780,000.

On September 19, 1999, the International House of Prayer in Kansas City, Missouri, started a worship-based prayer meeting that has continued for twenty-four hours a day, seven days a week ever since. With a similar vision to Moses, Samuel, King David, and Zinzendorf, that the fire on the altar should never go out, there has never been a time when worship and prayer has not ascended to heaven since that date.

At the same time, in many other places around the world, God placed desires and plans for 24/7 prayer in the fabric of diverse ministries and in the hearts of leaders. This has resulted in 24/7 houses of prayer and prayer mountains being established in every continent of the earth. The Columbus House of Prayer (CoHOP) of which I am affiliated, has answered the call to agree with heaven's mandate of 24/7 prayer and worship.

As we fast approach the coming of the Lord, God is expediting His ultimate will for earth to become like heaven, through day and night prayer. He prophesied through the Prophet Amos and confirmed it by the mouth of James, the brother of our Lord Jesus, that in these last days He will rebuild the 'Tabernacle of David' and restore the Davidic order of worship described above (24/7 intercessory worship, also known in many places as the "Harp and Bowl" described in Rev. 4).

Amos 9:11: *"In that day will I raise up the tabernacle of David that is fallen, and close up the breaches thereof; and I will raise up his ruins, and I will build it as in the days of old."*

Acts 15: 16 & 17: *"After this I will return, and will build again the tabernacle of David, which is fallen down; and I will build again the ruins thereof, and I will set it up: That the residue of men might seek after the Lord, and all the Gentiles, upon whom my name is called, saith the Lord, who doeth all these things."*

I believe that the major reason why sin, sickness, poverty, depravity, and even death does not, and cannot exist in heaven is because the Glory of God so much permeates and pervades heaven's atmosphere as a result of the continuous prayer and worship there. If we want similar results here on earth, which is

God's will, why don't we pray and ask God to replicate here what is done in heaven? God wants to unleash His Glory and Beauty upon our land and lives through prayer, which will eradicate every sin, disease, poverty, and death itself. Like Jesus taught His disciples, we need to pray "Let your will be done in the earth, as it is done in Heaven".

LET US PRAY:

Heavenly Father, I am so honored and privileged that you would reveal to me your will being done in heaven; with the intention that it would also be done here on earth. I acknowledge your desire for earth to reflect heaven. Help me to give myself, like your servant David, to day and night worship and prayer; because you are so worth it. I pray that you continue to raise up your Houses of Prayer in the earth, so that the knowledge of your glory will indeed fill the earth as the waters cover the sea (Hab 2:14). Please allow me to have a daily encounter with you as You open my eyes to behold Your Beauty, Splendor, and Holiness. Let your will be done on earth and in my life, as it is done in heaven. Amen!

CHAPTER 5

Prayer of Petition

(Connecting to Divine Provision)

Give us day by day our daily bread... (Luke 11:3)

After focusing the first few prayers on God's needs, Jesus begins to put the emphasis on our needs; and how through prayer we can have divine intervention to meet those needs. He particularly made sure that His disciples understood that this prayer was based on a daily communion with their Father. They were required to ask God to meet 'today's need'. Since bread was then, and still is now, the most common staple in the Middle Eastern diet accessible to anyone irrespective of their socio-economic status, Jesus used this most essential and common commodity to express the willingness of the Father to provide for his children's most mundane needs. He is not a Father who is only able to meet what we might consider being major needs, but will also satisfy us with our daily essential needs such as food, clothing, and shelter. In fact Jesus admonished us not to give into anxiety about these needs, knowing very well that our Heavenly Father is up to the task of taking care of his children (Matt. 6:25-34).

As we have stated earlier, God our Father is definitely interested and willing to meet all our needs and desires. He revealed Himself to Abraham, our father through faith, as "Jehovah-Jireh" which means,

> *The first principle in receiving God's provision is asking.*

"The Lord who provides". There are several scriptures that describe God's absolute and unwavering willingness to hear, answer, and thus release provision to His children who simply ask or petition Him.

Matt. 7:7-8: *"Ask, and it shall be given you; seek, and ye shall find; knock, and it shall be opened unto you: **For every one that asketh receiveth；** and he that seeketh findeth; and to him that knocketh it shall be opened."* (Emphasis mine)

However, He has set things up such that we receive His provision only when we ask or pray. In other words, the first principle to receiving God's provision is by asking. The Epistle of James gives us two basic reasons we do not receive provision for our needs.

James 4:2-3: *"Ye lust, and have not: ye kill, and desire to have, and cannot obtain: ye fight and war,* **yet ye have not, because ye ask not***. Ye ask, and receive not,* **because ye ask amiss***, that ye may consume it upon your lusts."* (Emphasis mine)

The Silent Treatment:

The first reason we do not receive provision for our needs is simply because we do not ask God for it. Many people go through life without verbalizing their requests or petitions to God; and yet wonder and become disappointed or disillusioned with Him for the lack of provision in their lives. They wrongly assume that God, being sovereign and good, is automatically moved by their need and hence expect quick intervention. It is a true statement that God is not moved by your or my needs. If He was moved just by needs, there would not be a need in anybody's life in the world. He is compassionate towards our needs, but will not violate His own principle that He has set forth concerning the connection between His provision and the prayers of His children. God is ONLY moved to intervene with His provision when you and I ask for His provision in faith… believing.

Stop Complaining; PRAY!

There are also those who even though they verbalize their need do not receive results and also wonder why. It is unfortunate that many substitute complaining about their situation for real prayer. Complaining or "fussing" about your need is not the same as praying or asking God for His provision. Once again, God is not moved by our complaining and weeping. On the contrary, this attitude rather offends Him and engenders His displeasure and disapproval. This attitude of complaining will lead to further prolonging of the time we would have to endure the circumstance, or lack the thing which we need provision for.

This was the experience of the nation of Israel as they exited the land of bondage (by the outstretched Hand of God) and found themselves in the Wilderness without food or water. Instead of trusting in God's promise and providence, they resorted to murmuring and complaining against God and His chosen leadership. This attitude resulted in immediate retribution as many died, and also long term disappointment as they had a longer than expected "layover" in the wilderness. A journey that was supposed to last them about eleven days took them forty years to accomplish because their complaint and murmuring caused them to circumvent the same mountain over and over again. The Apostle Paul admonished the Church in Corinthians (and us) to take the experience of the Israelites as an example:

1 Cor. 10:1-5: *"Moreover, brethren, I would not that ye should be ignorant, how that all our fathers were under the cloud, and all passed through the sea; And were all baptized unto Moses in the cloud and in the sea; And did all eat the same spiritual meat; And did all drink the same spiritual drink: for they drank of that spiritual Rock that followed them: and that Rock was Christ.* ***But with many of them God was not well pleased: for they were overthrown in the wilderness.***" (Emphasis mine)

1 Cor. 10:10 & 11: *"Neither murmur ye, as some of them also murmured, and were destroyed of the destroyer.* ***Now all these things happened unto them for ensamples: and they are written for our admonition, upon whom the ends of the world are come.***" (Emphasis mine)

The story of Habakkuk exemplifies this attitude of complaining which many substitute for real prayer. A brief summary of the three chapters of the Book of Habakkuk is helpful to understand how the Prophet of God transitioned from a position of complaint to a position of petition, and what the response of God was to both positions.

The first chapter of the book narrates the terrible circumstances that the people of God were under as a direct result of their own sin and rebellion against God and His laws. This state of affairs was unacceptable to the Prophet, and hence he went into a tirade of complaints against God using the words "why" and "how" to question God for the situation of the people, (Habakuk 1:2 & 3). God's initial response to His Prophet in so many words was that they were under His judgment, and something worse was even in the pipeline; He was about to use a cruel and wicked nation to execute the second phase of their judgment, (Hab. 1:5-9). In other words, as long as Habakkuk complained the situation did not improve, but either remained or grew worse. Joyce Meyer puts it this way, "When you complain, you remain; but when you praise God in the midst of your situation, He will raise you out of it".

Habakkuk finally decided to change his posture from complaining into one of praying, because in chapter 2 he says, "I will stand upon my watch, and set me upon the tower, and will watch to see what he will say unto me..." (Hab. 2:1). Standing upon his watch implies prayer, similar to what Jesus told us to do: to watch and pray. This

> *When you complain, you remain; when you praise you will be raised.*

posture elicited a different response from God. It was an awesome response, because God suddenly gave him a vision of the outcome of the crisis His people were facing. This was the answer, breakthrough, or provision that Habakkuk needed all this while, but would not have received if he maintained his position of complaining rather than actually praying and waiting on God's response.

We need to learn from Habakkuk's experience. It does us no good to complain in times of difficulty and lack. Even though we may not understand the "why, how, and when", we need to trust in God's unfailing love and talk to Him about the answer or solution to the problem; instead of rehearsing and focusing on the problem. He said if you will simply ASK, then you will RECEIVE. It's as simple as that!

Praying Amiss:

The second reason James gives for our lack of provision to our needs is that even though many may be asking, they "ask amiss". In other words, we miss the target with our petitions or requests. Even though I believe there are many reasons why many of us "pray amiss" and thus miss out on God's supernatural provisions, James gives an important one, which is; improper motives for our requests. According to him, asking God for something simply to satisfy a selfish, lustful, and carnal desire will not receive the desired response from God. In other words, our motives matter when we are praying the 'prayer of petition'. This brings us to one of the criteria Jesus Himself gave to receiving answers to our prayers; that is praying according to the will of God.

My Daily Bread:

What are some of the things that might constitute our daily bread which we are admonished to pray for? I believe the first and most important item on our list is the Word of God. The Word of God is referred to in many places in scripture as "bread". This is because it has the same attributes and effects in the spiritual life of the believer as bread does to the physical life. It is essential to the growth and health of the believer; and also accessible to anyone irrespective of age, gender, or socio-economic status.

One of the first and important miracles God did for His people Israel in their Wilderness experience to demonstrate His desire and ability to provide for their daily need was when He rained bread, known to them as "Manna", from heaven every morning. They were nourished and sustained daily for forty years on bread from heaven. Even though their physical sustenance was important to God, He was also giving them, and us today, a picture of how we need to be daily nourished and

> *Jesus is the Bread of Life!*

sustained spiritually. In fact, He made that connection to them, which Jesus repeated when He dealt with Satan in His own Wilderness experience:

Deut. 8:3: *"And he humbled thee, and suffered thee to hunger, and fed thee with manna, which thou knewest not, neither did thy fathers know;* **that he might make thee know that man doth not live by bread only, but by every word that proceedeth out of the mouth of the LORD doth man live."** (Emphasis mine)

Luke 4:3 & 4: *"And the devil said unto him, If thou be the Son of God, command this stone that it be made bread. And Jesus answered him, saying,* **It is written, That man shall not live by bread alone, but by every word of God."** (Emphasis mine)

Jesus, who is the Word of God made Flesh (John 1:14), in one of His discourses with His disciples confirmed that He was the "Bread of Life" that came from Heaven to nourish and sustain their fathers in the wilderness; and hence if they also wanted to be sustained they had to eat His Body.

John 6:31 - 35: *"Our fathers did eat manna in the desert; as it is written, He gave them bread from heaven to eat. Then Jesus said unto them, Verily, verily, I say unto you, Moses gave you not that bread from heaven; but my Father giveth you the true bread from heaven. For the bread of God is he which cometh down from heaven, and giveth life unto the world. Then said they unto him, Lord, evermore give us this bread. And Jesus said unto them,* **I am the bread of life**: *he that cometh to me shall never hunger; and he that believeth on me shall never thirst."* (Emphasis mine)

It is very clear that Jesus was referring to the Word of God and not to His physical body. If the people will partake daily of His 'body' they would be sustained spiritually and physically. If we will also commune with the Lord daily through prayer and His Word, we will be strengthened (Psalm 104:15), healed (Prov. 3:5), and directed (Psalm 119:105).

The second connotation of our "daily bread" is healing; physically, emotionally, spiritually, or socially. The subject of Healing has been a controversial subject in many circles in the Body of Christ. There are many arguments for and against whether healing is God's will for us, His children today. We will not attempt to answer all the questions about this subject in this book; however, let it suffice us to say that Jesus relegated healing as an essential and easily accessible provision from God to His children. He made it unequivocally clear that healing was the 'children's bread' in His dialogue with a Syrophenician woman whose daughter lay in bed oppressed by demonic spirits.

Mark 7:25 – 27: *"For a certain woman, whose young daughter had an unclean spirit, heard of him, and came and fell at his feet: The woman was a Greek, a Syrophenician by nation; and she* *besought him that he would cast forth the devil out of her daughter. But Jesus said unto her, Let the children first be filled:* **for it is not meet to take the children's bread***, and to cast it unto the dogs."* (Emphasis mine)

Note that Jesus clearly referred to the healing or deliverance for the girl as "bread" especially reserved for the children, which you and I are if we have been born again. Jesus was moved by the attitude and response of this woman who was foreign to the covenant of God, and thus unqualified to receive the "bread of the children".

Mark 7:28: *"And she answered and said unto him, Yes, Lord: yet the dogs under the table eat of the* ***children's crumbs****"* (Emphasis mine)

It is remarkable that she understood that even the "crumbs" had enough power to deliver her sick and demonized daughter. No wonder Jesus had any choice but to release virtue to deliver her daughter on account of her "great faith". My question to you and me, who are children of God and partakers of the covenant of grace, is if the 'bread crumbs' could bring total healing and deliverance to an unqualified seeker; how much more would the whole 'loaf of bread' bring healing and deliverance to us who qualify?

Your Heavenly Father is offended when you believe He is unwilling or incapable of giving you a most common, essential, and accessible commodity like healing or deliverance from demonic oppression. All he requires from you is to ask for daily bread or healing, and expect that it will be done. After all isn't that what we expect from our natural fathers? Which father will refuse his child toast or cereal in the morning?

Luke 11:11-13: *"If a son shall ask bread of any of you that is a father, will he give him a stone? or if he ask a fish, will he for a fish give him a serpent? Or if he shall ask an egg, will he offer him a scorpion?* **If ye then, being evil, know how to give good gifts unto your children: how much more shall your heavenly Father give the Holy Spirit to them that ask him?"** (Emphasis mine)

We should never doubt our Father's commitment to give us our "daily bread"; neither should we be amazed or surprised when He does, because that's who He is and what He does best: meeting the needs of His children.

LET US PRAY:

Father, thank you for the revelation that you are willing and able to provide all my needs, according to your riches in Christ Jesus. You are indeed my sustainer. Forgive me for the times when I have doubted your provision by either complaining instead of simply asking you, or being silent. You have taught me that just as earthly fathers give what their children ask of them, you being a more righteous Father will no doubt give me exactly what I need and ask for. Therefore, I thank you for providing my daily bread, including food, clothing, shelter, healing, etc. Father, by your grace, I will not be anxious for anything, but in everything, by prayer and supplication with thanksgiving, I will make my requests (petitions) known to you and thus receive your peace which surpasses human understanding. Allow that peace to keep my mind and heart through Jesus Christ. Amen!

CHAPTER 6
Prayer of Confession
(Connecting to Divine Pardon)

And forgive us our sins; for we also forgive every one that is indebted to us… (Luke 11:4a)

Andrew Murray aptly states, "As bread is the first need of the body, so forgiveness is to the soul." Forgiveness is one of the most, if not the most, important subject in the bible. In fact, our whole redemption and salvation is based on the forgiveness of a loving God toward a wayward people. Forgiveness is the gate through which all of God's redemptive blessings flow. If the gate is shut, no blessing is released no matter how much screaming we may do; but as soon as that gate swings open, the blessing of God is allowed to gush out.

The reason forgiveness is so important is because the only thing that stands between us and a vibrant and blessed relationship with a Holy God is the three letter word we all have in common, and yet no one wants to talk about any more in the church - SIN.

King David and the Prophet Isaiah actually make us to understand that the one obstacle that prevents us from receiving answers to our prayers is our sin.

Psalm 66:18: *"If I regard iniquity in my heart, the Lord will not hear me."*

Is. 59:1-2: *"Behold, the LORD'S hand is not shortened, that it cannot save; neither his ear heavy that it cannot hear: But your iniquities have separated between you and your God, and your sins have hid his face from you, that he will not hear."*

It is no wonder Jesus made sure he always included the subject of forgiveness in any teaching on prayer which He did. Without forgiveness, prayer will be ineffective, and hence the power of God will not be released to affect the needs of His people. In fact it is interesting to note that the only theme Jesus re-emphasized directly after His teaching on prayer was the theme on forgiveness.

Matt. 6:12-15: *"And forgive us our debts, as we forgive our debtors. And lead us not into temptation, but deliver us from evil: For thine is the kingdom, and the power, and the glory, for ever. Amen.* **For if ye forgive men their trespasses, your heavenly Father will also forgive you: But if ye forgive not men their trespasses, neither will your Father forgive your trespasses."* (Emphasis mine)

Mark 11:25 – 26: *"And when ye stand praying, forgive, if ye have ought against any: that your Father also which is in heaven may forgive you your trespasses. But if ye do not forgive, neither will your Father which is in heaven forgive your trespasses."*

This is how important and serious Jesus viewed the issue of forgiveness that He felt it was worth repeating. I believe too many believers, including Christian leaders, have not taken this admonishing from Jesus as serious as He desires it to be. Could it be that the reason the Church seems anemic and powerless in spite of all our prayers is because we have not heeded to Jesus' instruction on forgiveness? Don't we carry around with us bitterness, offenses, and un-forgiveness towards our brothers and sisters? Is un-forgiveness not one of the main reasons separation and/or divorce in Christian marriages is as high, if not higher, than those in the world? Is offense, bitterness, and un-forgiveness not the reason for many Church breakups and membership reallocations?

> *Forgiveness is the gate through which all of God's redemptive blessings flow.*

In His teaching on prayer, Jesus gives us two levels on which forgiveness is important: the forgiveness from God and the forgiveness from one another.

Forgive us:

As we have stated already, forgiveness from God is one of the most important gifts we can ever receive from Him. It is the reason Jesus died and resurrected from the dead; so that sinful man would be redeemed and restored back to righteousness (right-standing) with God.

Col. 1:13 -14: *"Who hath delivered us from the power of darkness, and hath translated us into the kingdom of his dear Son: In whom we have redemption through his blood, even the forgiveness of sins."*

Receiving God's forgiveness should be the greatest desire of every human being, since without it we are condemned to a life of damnation and eternal separation from God in Hell. The Bible clearly states that we have all sinned and hence are candidates for the wrath of God, (Rom. 3:23). Thus, receiving God's forgiveness should engender the greatest appreciation and reciprocal love back to God, setting one's heart ablaze in service to God and His Kingdom. The Psalmist really summed up the blessedness of the one whose sins are forgiven him or her; and how with a grateful heart the recipient of such blessing should respond.

Psalm 32:2: *"Blessed is the man unto whom the Lord imputes not iniquity, and in whose spirit there is no guile"*

Psalm 103: 2 & 3: *"Bless the LORD, O my soul, and forget not all His benefits:* **who forgives all your iniquities**, *and heals all your diseases"* (Emphasis mine)

However, this is not always the case since we either do not really understand what it means to be forgiven; or we simply take it for granted. I suggest the former is more accurate, since that was my case.

Growing up as a religious Catholic boy, I did my best to stay out of trouble and restrained from engaging in any "sinful" activities. Back then, and even now, sin was classified as "big" and "small"; hence more emphasis was put on the "big" sins which were categorized into the 'big 3':

    1. Sexual sins (fornication or adultery)

2. Drinking, and smoking (including drug abuse)
3. Murder

Since I stayed away (for the most part) from these sins, I was considered to be "righteous" among my peers; and I thought so too. Even though I faithfully went to church every Sunday, I still lacked the passion for God and the relationship with God that I saw and heard people speak about. I wondered why I couldn't be as passionate and in love with Jesus as these people. The only conclusion I could come up with was that every one of these men or women of God I wanted to emulate, because of their love and passion for God had a "testimony" of how Jesus forgave and delivered them from a past of wanton living. Their testimony was that they were fornicators, drunkards, drug addicts, Warlocks, and the like before Jesus saved them. I even considered the Apostle Paul, how he was a murderer before his encounter with Jesus on the road to Damascus. I therefore concluded that there was no way I was going to have such passion and power like these men and women without a testimony like theirs. I felt that my sins were not great enough to warrant enough of God's forgiveness to generate enough gratitude in my heart to love Him passionately. Little did I know that I was operating under the greatest sin; self-righteousness, which had made me prideful, judgmental, and self-conceited.

As I pondered upon my predicament; my inability to muster enough passion for God due to my self-righteousness, the Lord graciously opened my eyes to see the error in my suppositions. My problem was not in measuring how much sin I had committed or not; but rather having a revelation of how much I had been forgiven.

> *Having passion for God is based on your revelation and perspective on how much He has forgiven you.*

My predicament was the same predicament the Pharisees and the religious elite in Jesus' day had. They had a form of godliness and outward righteousness, but were disconnected from the reality of God's presence at the heart level. Jesus confronted this issue head on one day when He sat at dinner in one of the Pharisee's house.

Luke 7:36 – 48: *"And one of the Pharisees desired him that he would eat with him. And he went into the Pharisee's house, and sat down to meat. And, behold, a woman in the city, which was a sinner, when she knew that Jesus sat at meat in the Pharisee's house, brought an alabaster box of ointment, And stood at his feet behind him weeping, and began to wash his feet with tears, and did wipe them with the hairs of her head, and kissed his feet, and anointed them with the ointment. Now when the Pharisee which had bidden him saw it, he spake within himself, saying, This man, if he were a prophet, would have known who and what manner of woman this is that toucheth him: for she is a sinner. And Jesus answering said unto him, Simon, I have somewhat to say unto thee. And he saith, Master, say on. There was a certain creditor which had two debtors: the one owed five hundred pence, and the other fifty. And when they had nothing to pay, he frankly forgave them both. Tell me therefore, **which of them will love him most?** Simon answered and said, I suppose that he, **to whom he forgave most**. And he said unto him, Thou hast rightly judged. And he turned to the woman, and said unto Simon, Seest thou this woman? I entered into thine house, thou gavest me no water for my feet: but she hath washed my feet with tears, and wiped them with the hairs of her head. Thou gavest me no kiss: but this woman since the time I came in hath not ceased to kiss my feet. My head with oil thou didst not anoint: but this woman hath anointed my feet with ointment. Wherefore I say unto thee, Her sins, which are many, are forgiven; for she loved much: **but to whom little is forgiven, the same loveth little**. And he said unto her, Thy sins are forgiven."* (Emphasis mine)

This story changed my life forever! The truth is, having passion for God is based on your revelation and perspective on how much He has forgiven you. If you think you have been forgiven little because you discount the level of your sinfulness, you will love little like the Pharisees. However, if you know that the same amount of blood Jesus shed on the cross on behalf of that criminal next to Him was also shed for you, you will give your heart in love to Him like the woman who washed His feet with her tears and anointed Him with her most precious ointment. Jesus told the Pharisee, "He who is forgiven little, will love little; and he who is forgiven much, will love much."

When the Holy Spirit revealed this to me, I was liberated to love Him passionately; because for the first time in my life I realized how much God had forgiven me, and still forgives me. I came to the realization that even though I may not have acted out many of my sinful desires, I was as sinful, if not more, as these men and women whose love and passion for God I wanted to emulate. The only difference was that, whereas they recognized how much God had forgiven them; I was blinded by my own pride and self-righteousness which therefore kept my heart dull and unresponsive to God's passionate love for me. If you lack passion for God, after being saved for no matter how long, I suggest that you go down on your knees and ask the Lord to reveal to you how much you deserved to go to Hell, and how much He has forgiven you through the shed blood of Jesus on Calvary's cross.

Forgive "AS" You are forgiven:

Jesus set the standard of how the Father will deal with us in relation to forgiveness on how we deal with one another. If we are going to experience all that God has planned for us in this age, it will be wise to heed to the counsel of the Prince of Peace through whose blood we have redemption and the forgiveness of sins (Col. 1:14).

Jesus in His teaching said we should "forgive as we are forgiven". This reveals two aspects of forgiveness:

I. Quantity of Forgiveness:

God will forgive us just as many times we are willing to forgive those who do us wrong. Many of us don't have a problem forgiving someone for an offense they commit the first time. However, if they commit that same offense again, we are ready to throw down the gauntlet and make sure they forever owe us a debt.

Jesus dealt with this attitude when Peter asked Him a question about how many times he was required to forgive an offense.

Matt. 18:21: *"Then came Peter to him, and said, Lord, how oft shall my brother sin against me, and I forgive him? till seven times? Jesus saith unto him, I say not unto thee, Until seven times: but, Until seventy times seven."*

Peter in asking this question thought he was doing something very honorable by forgiving someone seven times for the same offense. You have to understand that the standard in those days under the Law of Moses was "an eye for an eye, and a tooth for a tooth". No one was under obligation to forgive any one for their sin against them; hence for Peter to even suggest forgiving someone seven times for an offense is remarkable and commendable. However, just like He did with the Sermon on the Mount (Matt. 5), Jesus raised the standard of righteousness to God's level. According to Jesus, seven times is not the standard, but seventy times seven which equals four hundred and ninety times. Simply put, if someone offends you every day of the year you should not run out of forgiveness.

II. Quality of Forgiveness:

The second aspect of forgiveness Jesus implies is the quality of our forgiveness. God will forgive us with the same quality of forgiveness we afford to each other. Jesus put it this way.

Luke 6:37 & 38: *"Judge not, and ye shall not be judged: condemn not, and ye shall not be condemned: **forgive, and ye shall be forgiven:** Give, and it shall be given unto you; good measure, pressed down, and shaken together, and running over, shall men give into your bosom. **For with the same measure that ye mete withal it shall be measured to you again.**"* (Emphasis mine)

Many times our forgiveness lacks sincerity. It is often times more of a lip-service than a heartfelt release of the offending person. We often justify this attitude with the saying, "I will forgive but won't forget." Even though we say we have forgiven the person, we find it difficult to relate well with the person and will refuse to assist them if we have the opportunity to do so. How would we feel if God took the same attitude with us? What if God also said "I forgive you but will not forget what you have done" Would there be enough books in heaven to keep an account of all our sins? But alas, God declares that when He forgives, He forgets.

In fact, He says He will not remember our sins and iniquities no more. At the end of Jesus' discourse about forgiveness with Peter and the other disciples, Jesus declared in

Matthew 18:33-35*: "Shouldest not thou also have had compassion on thy fellowservant, even as I had pity on thee? And his lord was wroth, and delivered him to the tormentors, till he should pay all that was due unto him.* **So likewise shall my heavenly Father do also unto you, if ye from your hearts forgive not everyone his brother their trespasses.***"* (Emphasis mine)

This necessitates the grace of God since no one in his or her own ability and willpower can achieve this standard of showing mercy. I believe this is why Jesus placed this aspect of prayer towards the end, because you would have had an encounter with the Father by now if you were following the model of prayer sequentially. It takes the Love of God to love others, so we need to ask the Father to help us forgive others as much as and with the same passion He forgives us.

LET US PRAY:

Father, I thank you for your revelation that forgiveness is the key to unlocking all your promises in my life. Without your forgiveness, I am locked out of your providence and grace. You have also let

me know, that your forgiveness towards me depends on my forgiveness towards all who have done me wrong. Father, please forgive me for holding any offense or grudge against anyone. I ask you for your grace to help me forgive those that have or will hurt me. Deliver me from the spirit of pride and offense; and release in me the ability to forgive my offenders and also to ask forgiveness of those I offend. As I walk in forgiveness, I thank you that your goodness and mercy abundantly overflow in and through my life. I am empowered to forgive AS I am forgiven. Amen!

CHAPTER 7

Prayer of Covering

(Connecting to Divine Protection)

And lead us not into temptation; but deliver us from evil.

(Luke 11:4)

I believe this prayer is one the most important, and yet difficult to understand. This is because Jesus gives us the impression that God will lead us into temptation unless we ask Him to do otherwise. The Bible makes it clear that God Himself cannot be tempted of evil, and does not tempt us with evil.

James 1:13-15: *"Let no man say when he is tempted, I am tempted of God:* **for God cannot be tempted with evil, neither tempteth he any man**: *But every man is tempted, when he is drawn away of his own lust, and enticed. Then when lust hath conceived, it bringeth forth sin: and sin, when it is finished, bringeth forth death. Do not err, my beloved brethren."* (Emphasis mine)

Temptation to sin is a primary function of our own lustful desires in co-operation with the devil. The Lord deals with this area in the second portion of this prayer where He directs us to pray that we would be delivered from evil.

So what does it mean to pray, "Lead us not into temptation?" The word "temptation" used in this lesson in prayer has two main connotations. According to Strong's Hebrew and Greek Dictionary, it means to entice (to sin); but also to test, scrutinize, examine, or discipline. It therefore has the same meaning as that which the Apostle Peter describes as the trial of our faith.

1 Pet. 1:6 – 7: *"Wherein ye greatly rejoice, though now for a season, if need be, ye are in heaviness through manifold **temptations**: That the **trial of your faith**, being much more precious than of gold that perisheth, though it be tried with fire, might be found unto praise and honour and glory at the appearing of Jesus Christ."* (Emphasis mine)

James, the half brother of Jesus, makes the same connection in his letter, when he says in

James 1:2 & 3: *"My brethren, count it all joy when ye fall into divers **temptations**; Knowing this, that the **trying of your faith** worketh patience."* (Emphasis mine)

According to these two patriarchs of our Christian faith, trials and/or temptations are not such a bad thing. If that is the case why would Jesus ask us to pray to the Father not to lead us into them?

What it suggests to us is, though we are to embrace trials when they come our way, they are not something we should invite upon ourselves. Jesus and the first century Apostles made it clear that trials and tribulations are a part of the Christian experience, but nowhere in the scriptures does it say we should pray for them.

John 16:33: *"These things I have spoken unto you, that in me ye might have peace.* ***In the world ye shall have tribulation****: but be of good cheer; I have overcome the world."* (Emphasis mine)

On the contrary, we see Jesus in the Garden of Gethsemane praying to the Father to take away His cup of suffering in His greatest hour of trial and temptation. Even though Jesus ultimately triumphed over this test by submitting His will to the Father's eternal plan, we have an insight into why Jesus will tell us to pray not to be led into trial or temptation. This does not mean that we will not be tried or tested, because we will. However, we are assured that when the trials do come, God makes sure we are able to bear them and ultimately overcome them through His wisdom and strength.

1 Cor. 10:12: *"Wherefore let him that thinketh he standeth take heed lest he fall. There hath no temptation taken you but such as is* *common to man: but God is faithful, who will not suffer you to be tempted above that ye are able; but will with the temptation also make a way to escape, that ye may be able to bear it."*

God's Trial, the Devil's Temptation:

The two views of "temptation" come into direct focus when we realize that what was meant to simply be a trial or test will be used by the devil as a temptation to entice us to sin. This is when a trial also becomes a temptation. God intends to use the trial to grow your faith if you co-operate with Him. At the same time the devil will use that same test to trigger your insecurities and lusts to cause you to fall.

> *Temptation to sin is a primary function of our own lustful desires in co-operation with the devil.*

For example, you may be going through a trial or test in the area of your finances. You may have lost your job and found yourself in a financial crisis where your sustenance is threatened. Foreclosure may be knocking on your door; and the car note has not been paid for months. This is definitely a trial of your faith you did not pray for nor hoped for. There are two forces at work in this crisis situation. You can either lean on God's word in 1 Corinthians 10:13 and trust that God has you covered and will provide you with a way of escape; or you can succumb to the devil's suggestions, playing on your fears and insecurities, to engage in an inappropriate behavior in order for you to get out of your predicament.

Many married couples have ended up in adulterous relationships simply because they succumbed to their own lustful desires, and the opportunities the devil created for them as a result of a

> *Be sober and vigilant in and out of season*

trial or problem in their marriage. Instead of going before the Lord in prayer and seeking godly counsel, they took what they assumed to be innocent solace in a friend of the opposite sex and before long, became unfaithful to their marital vows.

One thing the devil is good at is turning our trials into a temptation and then ultimately to a sin. That is one of the ways he has used to make casualty even some of the greatest giants of the faith. He comes in stealthily at our time of vulnerability during a trial and through suggestions cause us to lose our focus on God.

That is why the Bible tells us to always be sober and vigilant in and out of season because our enemy prowls around like a roaring lion; seeking someone to devour.

1 Pet. 5:8 – 9: *"Be sober, be vigilant; because your adversary the devil, as a roaring lion, walketh about, seeking whom he may devour: Whom resist stedfast in the faith, knowing that the same afflictions are accomplished in your brethren that are in the world."*

That is why Jesus teaches us to pray "lead us not into temptation, but deliver us from evil".

Keys to Victory:

1. Prayer

Prayer, and I mean a lifestyle of prayer, is the greatest tool God has provided us to not only overcome trials and temptations but also to detect them before they even come our way. Jesus showed us by example what to do before and during our time of trial or temptation. Before the greatest trial and temptation any man has had to encounter, our Lord went through the most intense prayer meeting any man has had to attend in the Garden of

Gethsemane. The Bible records that the Son of Man prayed until His sweat became drops of blood; and Angels had to be dispatched from Heaven to strengthen Him.

Luke 22:43 – 44: *"And there appeared an angel unto him from heaven, strengthening him. And being in an agony he prayed more earnestly: and his sweat was as it were great drops of blood falling down to the ground."*

Without this intense time of prayer, who knows if our Savior would have been able to endure the journey to the cross? The prayer not only strengthened Him, it also gave Him the perspective He needed to go through His trial. I believe it was during this time of engaging with His Father in prayer that the Bible says "He saw the joy that was set before Him", thus giving Him the fortitude and motivation to endure the cross. The Bible in that same passage in Hebrews reminds us and admonishes us that unlike Jesus, we have not yet resisted sin to the point of shedding blood, which Jesus did in the Garden of Gethsemane through prayer to overcome the temptation to sin.

Heb. 12:2-4: *"Looking unto Jesus the author and finisher of our faith; who for the joy that was set before him endured the cross, despising the shame, and is set down at the right hand of the* *throne of God. For consider him that endured such contradiction of sinners against himself, lest ye be wearied and faint in your minds.* ***Ye have not yet resisted unto blood, striving against sin.****"* (Emphasis mine)

If Jesus, who is fully Man and fully God, needed to pray in order to resist and overcome His trial and temptation, how much more do you and me need to pray.

It is unfortunate that His trusted inner core of Disciples (who He took with Him to help Him in prayer) did not realize the seriousness of the moment. Jesus did not mince words about the purpose of their prayer meeting. He knew what they were about to face too. This prayer meeting was not just about His trial, but also theirs. They were about to face their greatest test yet, especially Peter, concerning their relationship with Him. Jesus therefore gave them the key to resist and overcome their temptation - prayer.

Luke 22:40: *"And when he was at the place, he said unto them,* ***Pray that ye enter not into temptation.****"* (Emphasis mine)

Of course, we know that unlike Jesus, these Disciples decided to sleep instead of pray. We also know the outcome of their decision. While Jesus remarkably resisted and overcame His temptation and trial with grace and love; the disciples succumbed to their trial and deserted their Master. In the process Peter reacted violently and cut off a soldier's ear; 'cussed' out a young girl for questioning his association with Jesus; and denied Him three times. Could it be that these disciples would have also received Angelic assistance and strength like Jesus to resist the temptation that was to come if they had also prayed like their Master?

In fairness to Peter, Jesus had already forewarned him of Satan's request to sift him like wheat. However, Jesus gave Peter what I believe is one of the greatest revelations about His assignment and commitment to not just Peter, but also to us His disciples.

Luke 22:31 – 32: *"And the Lord said, Simon, Simon, behold, Satan hath desired to have you, that he may sift you as wheat:* ***But I have prayed for thee****, that thy faith fail not: and when thou art converted, strengthen thy brethren."* (Emphasis mine)

Just the thought that Jesus Himself is praying for me is amazing and reassuring. There are times during a trial or a temptation when you are too weak to pray. In those moments, you need to know beyond a shadow of doubt that there is One who is sitting at the Father's right Hand praying for you. He is our Great High Priest who is moved with the very feeling of our 'infirmities' or weaknesses and ever lives to make intercession for you and me.

Heb. 4:14 -16: *"Seeing then that we have a great high priest, that is passed into the heavens, Jesus the Son of God, let us hold fast our profession. For we have not an high priest which cannot be touched with the feeling of our infirmities; but was in all points tempted like as we are, yet without sin. Let us therefore come boldly unto the throne of grace, that we may obtain mercy, and find grace to help in time of need."*

Heb. 7:24 -25: *"But this man, because he continueth ever, hath an unchangeable priesthood. Wherefore he is able also to save them to the uttermost that come unto God by him, seeing he ever liveth to make intercession for them."*

It is also important to have other believers we are in fellowship with, pray with and for us, especially when trials and temptations come knocking on our door. Without such prayer covering, the Apostle Peter could have ended up with the same fate as the Apostle James who was beheaded by Herod. When the Church raised their voices in prayer on behalf of Peter who was in captivity awaiting execution the next day, an angel was dispatched to bring deliverance to the Apostle, (Acts 12).

If you are facing some form of trial or temptation right now, I encourage you to find you a prayer "closet" and engage the Father in prayer. He will either deliver you outright from the situation, like He did for Peter after the Church prayed, or deliver you like He did for Paul and Silas after they praised and prayed (Acts 16). If you are not delivered instantly, He will give you supernatural grace and strength to endure the test like He did for Jesus, Paul and the three Hebrew boys in the Book of Daniel, (2 Cor. 12:7-9).

2. Knowing God's Affections

One of the greatest ways to resist and overcome temptation is to know God's love and affection for you; and thus generating a reciprocal love and affection from us to Him. Walking in obedience to God's commands should be the Christian's highest priority and goal. According to Jesus, obedience is proof of our love. If you love Him then you will obey His commands, as He aptly put it to His disciples in John 14:15. There are three basic motivations that drive our desire and ability to walk in obedience to God, thus allowing us to overcome varying degrees of temptation.

i. Fear-Based Obedience:

This type of obedience is motivated by the fear of some form of consequence or punishment associated with the sinful desire or action. The fear of losing your marriage or your reputation may be the motivation behind you not engaging in that extra-marital affair. However, obedience motivated by fear, even though it is legitimate and biblical, is the least effective way to sustain a lifestyle of obedience. Those who rely on

> *Walking in obedience to God's commands should be the Christian's highest priority.*

such motivation to resist or overcome temptation invariably end up falling into the trap of the enemy's deception.

Many Christians got saved because of the fear of Hell being preached to them. However, the fear of Hell cannot remain the primary motivation to stay saved; because as the months and years prolong, the urgency of that fear ultimately wears off and that is one of the reasons some leave the faith altogether. For those who stay, it becomes a religious exercise devoid of a heartfelt connection with the Lord. If you are depending primarily on the fear of retribution to sustain your ability to say "no" to sin, the enemy knows how to eventually convince you that it is either not a big deal after all, or show you how you can get away with the action without being caught. We need to maintain a certain level of fear, because the consequence and retribution of Hell is real. However that cannot become our primary motivation.

ii. Faith/Duty-Based Obedience:

This type of obedience relies on the individual's personal determination to be faithful to the commands of the Lord irrespective of how they may feel. They take obedience to God's commands as a duty and feel obligated to honor them, even though they may not have a vibrant heartfelt relationship and fellowship with the Lord. Once again, as honorable, legitimate, and biblical this type of motivation may be it falls short on so many levels. Firstly and most importantly, it often gives rise to the spirit of

Pharisaism and legalism. This creates a false sense of superiority over others who may not be in compliance with a particular set of "rules" or commands. Jesus dealt with this spirit throughout His ministry on earth stressing to the Pharisees the importance of not only an outward adherence to the Law, but also an inward affection for God.

Matt. 15:6 – 9: *"...And honour not his father or his mother, he shall be free. Thus have ye made the commandment of God of none effect by your tradition. Ye hypocrites, well did Esaias prophesy of you, saying, This people draweth nigh unto me with their mouth, and honoureth me with their lips; but their heart is far from me. But in vain they do worship me, teaching for doctrines the commandments of men."*

Matt. 12:7: *"But if ye had known what this meaneth, I will have mercy, and not sacrifice; ye would not have condemned the guiltless."*

Secondly, for those who do not fall into the trap of the Pharisees, it becomes difficult for them to sustain a lifestyle of obedience primarily motivated by duty or faith. After a while, we are prone to give in to the constant barrage of the enemy's suggestions and the sheer weakness of our flesh. We were made by God to feel His love and tenderness towards us and vice-versa;

devoid of that, our journey of faith becomes arduous and unfulfilling. We end up walking with a sense of guilt, shame, and condemnation because we gave in to Satan's temptations after trying with all our might to resist him. We need to be reminded that "it is not by power or by might, but by My Spirit says the Lord" (Zech. 4:6).

iii. Affection-Based Obedience:

This type of obedience relies on the knowledge that God loves and has deep affections for the individual no matter their circumstance. This knowledge of God's love and affection triggers a reciprocal love and affection from the individual back to God. It is important to recognize that the only way you can truly have love for God is when His love for you becomes undeniably evident to you. The sons of Korah had one of the most profound prophecies concerning God's unquestionable desire and affection for His people, and how that affection stirs in us a desire to honor, respect, and walk in obedience towards Him.

Psalm 45:11: "The king is enthralled by your beauty; honor him, for he is your Lord." (NIV)

As you can see from the above scripture, what truly empowers us to honor God, through our obedience to Him, is a revelation and deep understanding that He is indeed enthralled, ravished, and affectionate towards us. It is amazing that most of us will not consider ourselves "beautiful" in the sight of God due to our various failings, weaknesses, inadequacies, and even sins. The accuser of the brethren, Satan, will make sure to remind you and me, if we let him; of our darkness and ugliness before God. However, if we will listen closely to the Father, we will hear Him say "you are still

> *We were made by God to feel His love and tenderness.*

beautiful to me; you are still the apple of my eye". Beauty indeed lies in the eyes of the beholder; and though others may not see it, God continually beholds you and me as beautiful. This revelation completely revolutionizes the way we view Him, and the way we view ourselves, especially where holiness is concerned. Holiness no longer becomes something to try to achieve out of fear or religious duty, but as a divine invitation to intimacy with the creator of the universe.

I truly believe that the level and extent of your love for God is directly correspondent to the level and extent of the revelation you have concerning His love for you. The more revelation you have about His love for you, the more love you have for Him. The Apostle of Love, John, puts it this way;

1 John 4:19: *"We love him, because he first loved us."*

This is what empowers you and me to sustain a lifestyle of obedience based absolutely on God's love; not on fear or duty. When we actually feel love from God and love for God, it is easy to say "No" to the temptations of the evil one through the mind and flesh.

The Psalmist also confirms that the reason God will deliver you and me from trials and temptations is because of the reciprocal relationship based on love.

Psalm 18:19: *"He brought me forth also into a large place; he delivered me, because he delighted in me."*

This Psalm was most probably written by David during one of the greatest trials of his life as a result of his illicit affair with Bathsheba and the subsequent murder of her husband Uriah. David could have been bent over with shame and condemnation, wallowing in doubt about how God felt about him. That kind of attitude would have surely caused him to just accept the challenging circumstances he faced, for after all he deserved it. The devil would have undoubtedly reminded him of what a mess he was and how undeserving he was of God's love and affection. However, David refused to see himself less than how God saw him. He still recognized that in spite of his sin, God still delighted in him and loved him especially since he had acknowledged, confessed, and repented of the sin. He understood that this affection and delight of God for him was the only reason why deliverance was assured.

> *We love him, because he first loved us*

No matter what sin you have committed, and as a result you are facing the bombardment of Satan's attacks, you cannot doubt that God still delights in you especially if you have acknowledged and repented of the sins. You have to see a God who is so passionate with love for you that he runs and embraces you with a smile on His face like He did for the Prodigal son in Luke 15. He will deliver you from your fierce trial. You just have to know that He delights in you; so set your affections on Him.

Psalm 91:14 & 15: *"Because he hath set his love upon me, therefore will I deliver him: I will set him on high, because he hath known my name. He shall call upon me, and I will answer him: I will be with him in trouble; I will deliver him, and honour him."*

There is a place for obedience motivated by fear; there is a place for obedience motivated by duty or faith; but the greatest motivation for walking in complete obedience to the Lord is love… reciprocal love. Prayer and knowing God's affections for you will anchor your soul in order for you to persevere through any and all trials and temptations. Pray today that He will deliver you from evil, and will lead you "not into temptation" (trial).

LET US PRAY:

Thank you Father for letting me know how much you love me and how much you desire to protect me and deliver me from every evil. Please strengthen me by your Spirit in my inward man, so that I will be able to resist the temptations of the devil. Give me discernment to know the way of escape you have provided for me in the midst of my trials. Father, I ask you for the Spirit of revelation to know you more and more, that as I encounter your beauty and love, I will also grow in love for you enabling me to walk in complete obedience toward you. Thank you that you lead me not into temptation and deliver me out of every evil. You are my protector and deliverer. Amen!

Epilogue

The following is an exposition of the various movements of prayer in history initiated by God in response to the desire of His heart to cause His will to be done in earth just as it is being done in heaven. It can be found on the International House of Prayer (IHOP-KC) website, (www.ihop.org.)

The Early Monastic Tradition of 24/7 Prayer

For over one thousand years monasticism (the practice of taking vows of poverty, chastity, and obedience to one's spiritual superior) held a key role in the development of theology and practice in the Church. From the fourth and fifth centuries, monks and nuns were an accepted part of society. Monasticism is the cradle from which laus perennis, perpetual prayer, was birthed in the church age. We will now discuss some of the key figures of this tradition.

Alexander Akimetes and the Sleepless Ones

Born in Asia Minor and educated in Constantinople, Alexander became an officer in the Roman army. Challenged by

Jesus' words to the rich young ruler from Mathew 19:21, Akimetes sold his possessions and retreated from court life to the desert. Tradition states that he set fire to a pagan temple after seven years of solitude. Upon arrest and imprisonment Alexander converted the prison governor and his household, and promptly returned to his abode in the desert. Shortly thereafter he had the misfortune to fall in with a group of robbers. His evangelistic zeal, however, could not be contained and he converted these outcasts into devoted followers of Jesus. This group became the core of his band of monks.

Around 400 AD, he returned to Constantinople with 300–400 monks, where he established laus perennis to fulfill Paul's exhortation to pray without ceasing (1 Thes 5:17). Driven from Constantinople, the monks established the monastery at Gormon, at the mouth of the Black Sea. This became the founding monastery of the order of the Acoemetae (literally, the sleepless ones). Alexander died here in 430 AD, but the influence of the Acoemetae continued. The houses were divided into six choirs rotating throughout the day, each new choir relieving the one before, to create uninterrupted prayer and worship twenty-four hours a day.

John, the second abbot of the Acoemetae, founded another monastery on the eastern shore of the Bosphorus, referred to in many ancient documents as the "great monastery" and motherhouse of the Acoemetae. The library here was recognized for its greatness throughout the Byzantine Empire and indeed was consulted by several popes. The third abbot established a monastery in the capital under the royal consul, Studius, who dedicated the new monastery to John the Baptist. Studion became a renowned center of learning and piety, the most important monastery in Constantinople. Studion continued until 1453 when the Turks captured Constantinople.

The lasting impact of the Acoematae has been their worship and their contribution to church liturgy. The monasteries, numbering into the hundreds and sometimes thousands, were organized into national groups of Latins, Greeks, Syrians, and Egyptians, and then into choirs. In addition to laus perennis, which passed into the Western Church with St. Maurice of Agaune, they developed the Divine Office—the literal carrying out of Psalm 119:164, "Seven times a day I praise You, because of Your righteous judgments." This became an integral part of the Benedictine rule of the seven hours of prayer—Matins, Lauds, Prime, Terce, Sext, None, Vespers, and Compline.

Agaunum

Around 522 AD, Abbot Ambrosius brought attention to a small monastery founded in Switzerland. Legend has it that around 286 AD, a Theban Legion under the command of Maurice de Valois was sent to suppress a rebellion by Gauls in the north of the empire. On their way to Gaul, the Coptic Christians were encamped at Agaunum (present-day Switzerland) where they were ordered to sacrifice to Roman gods and to the Emperor in petition for victory. Maurice and his Theban Legion refused. The Roman emperor, Maximian, ordered a "decimation" of the legion of seven thousand: one in every ten men was killed. When Maurice and his men continued their refusal, a second decimation was ordered, followed by another and another. The entire seven thousand Egyptian Christians were eventually martyred.

Although the veracity of the story has been called into question, the legend of the martyrs at Agaunum spread far and wide. Between 515 and 521 AD, Sigismund, King of Burgundy, lavishly endowed the monastery established at the site of the martyrdom to ensure its success. In 522 AD, the abbot at St. Maurice's instituted laus perennis after the tradition of the Acoemetae. Choirs of monks would sing in rotation, with one choir relieving the previous choir, continuing day and night. This practice went on until around 900 AD, impacting monasteries all over France and Switzerland.

Comgall and Bangor

The Mappa Mundi, the most celebrated of all medieval maps, contains reference to a place on the edge of the known world: Bangor, Ireland. Why was this small, out of the way place, now a dormant coastal town fifteen miles from Belfast, the capital of Northern Ireland, so important in medieval times?

St. Patrick and Vallis Angelorum

Monasticism in Britain and Ireland developed along similar lines to those of the Desert Fathers of the East. St. Patrick's mother was a close relative of Martin of Tours, a contemporary of St. Antony, the father of monasticism. It is no surprise that the same type of asceticism which accompanied the monastic lifestyle in Egypt was also found in Ireland.

In 433 AD, just as the Roman Empire was starting to crumble, St. Patrick returned to Ireland (having been enslaved on the island previously) with a view to preaching the Christian message to the Irish. He was followed by a number of other ascetics—Finnian, Brigid, and Ciaran, all of whom established monastic centers throughout the island. While Christianity in much of the empire had been founded upon bishops overseeing cities and urban centers, Ireland had never been conquered and had no urban centers. The fall of the empire therefore had little impact on it, making it relatively easy for monasteries to become the center of influence in Irish society.

According to the twelfth century Anglo-Norman Monk Jocelin, Patrick came to rest in a valley on the shores of the Belfast Lough on one of his many journeys. Here, he and his comrades beheld a vision of heaven. Jocelin states: "they held the valley filled with heavenly light, and with a multitude of heaven, they heard, as chanted forth from the voice of angels, the psalmody of the celestial choir." The place became known as the Vallis Angelorum or the Vale of Angels. The famed Bangor Monastery would begin its life here approximately one hundred years later; from this spot, heaven's song would reach into Europe.

Introducing Comgall

Bangor's founder, Comgall, was born in Antrim in 517 AD. Originally a soldier, he soon took monastic vows and was educated for his new life. He is next seen in the Irish annals as a hermit on Lough Erne. However, his rule was so severe that seven of his fellow monks died and he was persuaded to leave and establish a house at Bangor (or Beannchar, from the Irish Horned Curve, probably in reference to the bay) in the famed Vale of the Angels. The earliest Irish annals give 558 as the date of Bangor's commencement.

Bangor Mor and Perpetual Psalmody

At Bangor, Comgall instituted a rigid monastic rule of incessant prayer and fasting. Far from turning people away, this ascetic rule attracted thousands. When Comgall died in 602, the annals report that three thousand monks looked to him for guidance. Bangor Mor, named "the great Bangor" to distinguish it from its British contemporaries, became the greatest monastic school in Ulster as well as one of the three leading lights of Celtic Christianity. The others were Iona, the great missionary center founded by Colomba, and Bangor on the Dee, in Wales, founded by Dinooth; the ancient Welsh Triads also confirm the "Perpetual Harmonies" at this great house.

Throughout the sixth century, Bangor became famous for its choral psalmody; "It was this music which was carried to the Continent by the Bangor Missionaries in the following century" (Hamilton, Rector of Bangor Abbey). Divine services of the seven hours of prayer were carried out throughout Bangor's existence. However, the monks went further and carried out the practice of laus perennis. In the twelfth century, Bernard of Clairvaux spoke of Comgall and Bangor, stating, "The solemnization of divine offices was kept up by companies, who relieved each other in succession, so that not for one moment day and night was there an intermission of their devotions." This continuous singing was antiphonal in nature, based on the call and response reminiscent of Patrick's vision, but also practiced by St. Martin's houses in Gaul. Many of these psalms and hymns were later written down in the Antiphonary of Bangor which came to reside in Colombanus' monastery at Bobbio, Italy.

The Bangor Missionaries

The ascetic life of prayer and fasting was the attraction of Bangor. However, as time progressed, Bangor also became a famed seat of learning and education. There was a saying in Europe at the time that if a man knew Greek he was bound to be an Irishman, largely due to the influence of Bangor. The monastery further became a missions-sending community. Even to this day, missionary societies are based in the town. Bangor monks appear throughout medieval literature as a force for good.

> *The ascetic life of prayer and fasting was the attraction of Bangor.*

In 580 AD, a Bangor monk named Mirin took Christianity to Paisley, where he died "full of miracles and holiness." In 590, the fiery Colombanus, one of Comgall's leaders, set out from Bangor with twelve other brothers, including Gall who planted monasteries throughout Switzerland. In Burgundy he established a severe monastic rule at Luxeil which mirrored that of Bangor. From there he went to Bobbio in Italy and established the house which became one of the largest and finest monasteries in Europe. Colombanus died in 615, but by 700 AD, one hundred additional monasteries had been planted throughout France, Germany, and Switzerland. Other famed missionary monks who went out from Bangor include Molua, Findchua, and Luanus.

The End of Greatness

The greatness of Bangor came to a close in 824 with raids from the marauding Vikings; in one raid alone, 900 monks were slaughtered. Although the twelfth century saw a resurrection of the fire of Comgall initiated by Malachy (a close friend of Bernard of Clairvaux, who wrote The Life of St. Malachy), it unfortunately never had the same impact as the early Celtic firebrands who held back the tide of darkness and societal collapse by bringing God to a broken generation.

Cluny

In the ninth and tenth centuries, Viking raiders and settlers were forging a violent new way of life in Europe. Feudalism was taking root and the monastic way of life was shaken—not only by the physical attacks that Bangor experienced, but by the consequences of the raids, when many houses were subject to the whims of local chieftains. In reaction to this movement, reform came about in several ways, one arguably being the most crucial reforming movement in the Western Church: the Cluniac order.

In 910, William the Pious, Duke of Aquitaine, founded the monastery at Cluny under the auspices of Abbot Berno, instituting a stricter form of the Benedictine rule. William endowed the abbey with resources from his entire domain, but more importantly gave the abbey freedom in two regards. Due to the financial endowment, the abbey was committed to increased prayer and perpetual praise—in other words, laus perennis. Its autonomy from secular leadership was also important as the abbey was directly accountable to the church in Rome.

The second abbot, Odo, took over in 926. According to C. H. Lawrence, he was "a living embodiment of the Benedictine ideal." His reforming zeal meant that the influence of the monastery at Cluny expanded widely during his leadership. Known for its independence, hospitality and alms giving, Cluny significantly departed from the Benedictine rule, removing manual labor from a monk's day and replacing it with increased prayer. The number of monastic houses which looked to Cluny as their motherhouse increased greatly during this period, and the influence of the house spread all over Europe.

Cluny reached the zenith of its power and influence in the twelfth century; it commanded 314 monasteries all over Europe, second only to Rome in terms of importance in the Christian world. It became a seat of learning, training no less than four popes. The fast-growing community at Cluny necessitated a great need for buildings. In 1089, the abbey at Cluny began construction under Hugh, the sixth abbot. It was finished by 1132 and was considered to be one of the wonders of the Middle Ages. More than 555 feet in length, it was the largest building in Europe until St. Peter's Basilica was built in Rome during the sixteenth century. Consisting of five naves, a narthex (ante-church), several towers, and the conventual buildings, it covered an area of twenty-five acres. However, even before these great building projects, it is interesting to note that the decline in spirituality led to the ultimate demise of Cluny's influence.

Zinzendorf's Early Years

The Reformation of the sixteenth century saw much-needed reform enter the European church, which also caused the closing of many monasteries that had become spiritually dead. The next great champion of 24/7 prayer would not appear until the start of the eighteenth century—Count Nicholas Ludwig Von Zinzendorf.

Zinzendorf was born in 1700 to an aristocratic but pious family. His father died when he was only six weeks old. The young boy was therefore brought up by his grandmother, a well-known leader of the Pietist movement and friendly with the established leader of the Pietists and young Zinzendorf's godfather, Phillipp Spener. Growing up in the midst of such passion for Jesus, Zinzendorf speaks of his early childhood as a time of great piety: "In my fourth year I began to seek God earnestly, and determined to become a true servant of Jesus Christ."

From the age of ten, Zinzendorf was tutored at the Pietist school of Halle under the watchful eye of Augustus Francke, another leader of the Pietists. There he formed a school club which lasted all his life, The Honourable Order of the Mustard Seed. After several years at Halle, Zinzendorf's uncle considered the young count too much of a Pietist and had him sent to Wittenberg to learn jurisprudence, so that he might be prepared for court life. Soon the young count was accepted in various circles of society in Europe. He kept these connections for the rest of his life, although his position in the Dresden Court and future plans for Saxon court life as Secretary of State would not be fulfilled.

The Moravians and Herrnhut

In 1722, Zinzendorf bought the Berthelsdorf estate from his grandmother and installed a Pietist preacher in the local Lutheran church. That same year Zinzendorf came into contact with a Moravian preacher, Christian David, who persuaded the young count of the sufferings of the persecuted Protestants in Moravia. These Moravians known as the Unitas Fratrum were the remains of

John Huss's followers in Bohemia. Since the 1600s, these saints had suffered under the hands of successive repressive Catholic monarchs. Zinzendorf offered them asylum on his lands. Christian David returned to Bohemia and brought many to settle on Zinzendorf's estate, forming the community of Herrnhut, The Watch of the Lord. The community quickly grew to around three hundred, and, due to divisions and tension in the infant community, Zinzendorf gave up his court position and became the leader of the brethren, instituting a new constitution for the community.

The Hundred-Year Prayer Meeting & Subsequent Missions

A new spirituality now characterized the community, with men and women being committed to bands or choruses to encourage one another in the life of God. August of 1727 is seen as the Moravian Pentecost. Zinzendorf said August 13 was "a day of the outpourings of the Holy Spirit upon the congregation; it was its Pentecost." Within two weeks of the outpouring, twenty-four men and twenty-four women covenanted to pray "hourly intercessions," thus praying every hour around the clock. They were committed to see that, "The fire must be kept burning on the altar continuously; it must not go out" (Lev 6:13). The numbers committed to this endeavor soon increased to around seventy from the community. This prayer meeting would go non-stop for more than one hundred years and is seen by many as the spiritual power behind the impact the Moravians had on the world.

From the prayer room at Herrnhut came a missionary zeal which has hardly been surpassed in church history. The spark initially came from Zinzendorf's encounter in Denmark with Eskimos who had been converted by Lutherans. The count returned to Herrnhut and conveyed his passion to see the gospel go to the nations. As a result, many of the community went out into the world to preach the gospel, some even selling themselves into slavery in order to fulfill the great commission. This commitment is shown by a simple statistic. Typically, when it comes to world missions, the Protestant laity to missionary ratio has been 5000:1. The Moravians, however, saw a much increased ratio of 60:1. By 1776, some 226 missionaries had been sent out from the community at Herrnhut. It is clear through the teaching of the so-called father of modern missions, William Carey, that the Moravians had a profound impact on him in regard to their zeal for missionary activity. It is also through the missions-minded Moravians that John Wesley came to faith. The impact of this little community in Saxony, which committed to seek the face of the Lord day and night, has truly been immeasurable.

Biography

Alfred Tagoe is the founder of Voice of Revival Ministries, a non-denominational prayer ministry focused on bringing a genuine Holy Ghost Revival to the Body of Christ through prayer and the Word of God. As part of his mandate from God, he is the director of the Columbus House of Prayer (CoHOP), a Prayer, Worship, and Justice center where believers from every denomination and ethnic background come and contend for the Heart of God through day and night worship and prayer to bring regional transformation to our cities and nation (Is 56:7). He also hosts Prayer Summits which call the Body of Christ to a "solemn assembly" to cry before the Lord on behalf of our land that it will be healed (Joel 2:15). Finally, through the Nehemiah Project, he has been uniquely called and gifted apostolically to bring the message of prayer and revival to Churches and Regions to 'rebuild the walls and repair the gates' of our cities in order for the Glory of God to be revealed and released (Neh 2:5).

Alfred has served in many leadership roles, especially in the area of prayer, ever since God birthed a spirit of prayer and revival in his heart in 1994. He is a graduate of World Harvest Bible College with a diploma in Pastoral Studies; and Franklin University with a Bachelor of Science in Organizational Communication; and in the process of obtaining his Masters in Business Administration.

His passion is to witness the last great awakening and revival; and help the Body of Christ rediscover their original purpose of intimacy with their creator God, and His Son Jesus. His mission is to be a "forerunner" like John the Baptist to "prepare the way of the Lord" (Luke 3:4) and "make ready a people prepared for the Lord" (Luke 1:17). Alfred currently resides in Columbus, Ohio with his lovely wife Angelina and three children Jezaniah, Jaeda, and Joshua

Contact Information

For more information about the Author, please write to:

Alfred Tagoe,
Voice of Revival Ministries,
5696 Earnings Dr, Columbus Ohio, 43232.
Tel: 614-312-2624
Email: alfredchrist01@gmail.com
www.facebook.com/alfred.christ
www.voiceofrevival.net

For more information about the Columbus House of Prayer (CoHOP), please visit website at www.columbushop.org

Or write to:
Alfred Tagoe
Columbus House of Prayer (CoHOP)
1673 Karl Court, Columbus Ohio, 43229
Tel: 614-5COHOP8 (614-526-4678)
Email: Director@columbushop.org

www.ingramcontent.com/pod-product-compliance
Lightning Source LLC
Chambersburg PA
CBHW070803100426
42742CB00012B/2236